Growing into Adolescence

*A Sensible Guide
For Parents of
Children 11 to 14*

Lynn Minton

Parents' Magazine Press
New York

International Standard Book Number 0–8193–0622–3
Library of Congress Catalog Card Number 73–190367
Produced for Parents' Magazine Press
by Stravon Educational Press
Manufactured in the United States of America

Contents

6 m 73 Parents Magazine Press $5.95

For Stu, Tim, Kathy, and Charlie
With love

THE AUTHOR IS grateful to Dr. Avrum H. Ben-Avi, Adjunct Professor of Psychology, New York University Graduate School of Arts and Sciences, and to Dr. Robert T. Porter, Associate Clinical Professor of Psychiatry, Mt. Sinai School of Medicine, for insights into the relationship between parents and children; and to Dr. Donald Gribetz, Clinical Professor of Pediatrics, Mt. Sinai School of Medicine, for his valuable assistance with sections of Chapter 7.

Special thanks to my husband, my parents, and my children, who were the source of many of the ideas in this book.

Preface

WHEN WE WERE in school, we were often told that these were "the best years of our lives." But most of us didn't believe it. When our children were babies, elderly ladies on the street would remonstrate with us not to look so harried because these were the best years of our lives. But there were too many diapers to change and too many eating schedules, there was too little time to read, and we were tired, and we didn't believe it then, either. But now that our children are growing into adolescence, life is more interesting. Now, *now* we can believe that these are the best years of our lives.

Only nobody says it any more, because everybody knows that living with children this age can be harrowing. It is, of course, but it can be immensely satisfying at the same time if we don't let the problems wear us down. That, in essence, is what this volume is all about. As we gain insight into what children of eleven to fourteen are experiencing, we become more able to perceive opportunities for mutual understanding and closeness, to forge during these years a rapport with our children that will form the basis of a rewarding lifelong relationship.

There will be ideas in these pages that simply do not fit your life or your child or that go against your grain. If a suggestion is not your style, ignore it. Use what you can, build on it, shape it to fit you exactly. The Bibliography can direct you to further reading in those areas of particular interest to you. The book is arranged so that one gets an idea of the physical and emotional changes that are typical of this age before moving on to the specific problems they can create. After reading the first two chapters, there is no strong reason not to skip around, dipping first into areas that intrigue you most or that are the most pressing, if you like to read that way.

If the use of "she" for parent and "he" for child grates, please accept that "he" for parent and "she" for child would be no more accurate, and saying "he or she" in every sentence would have driven you up the wall. So, if you and your husband (or you and your wife) are lucky enough to share equally in bringing up your children, we hope you and she (or you and he) will share this book, too. It is for both of you.

1
Suddenly: Adolescence

DEAR, DEAR! HOW queer everything is today! And yesterday things went on just as usual. I wonder if I've been changed in the night? Let me think: was I the same when I got up this morning? I almost think I can remember feeling a little different. But if I'm not the same, the next question is, Who in the world am I? Ah, *that's* the great puzzle!" said Alice.

"Explain yourself!" said the caterpillar.

"I can't explain *myself*, I'm afraid, sir," said Alice, "because I'm not myself, you see."

With overwhelming suddenness, Lewis Carroll's heroine of *Alice's Adventures in Wonderland* is propelled far from the warm and comfortable shores of her childhood. She finds herself in a strange land where nothing is familiar. Most frightening of all, she finds that she *isn't* any more, but exists only in an ephemeral state of *becoming*.

Surely that is a story of this time in the lives of our children when strong and inexorable forces inside

14

them thrust them toward adulthood. Their bodies change and grow faster than at any other time in their lives, except for their first year. But becoming an adult is not just a question of growing bigger. It involves a disruption of the entire functioning, physical, emotional, intellectual, of the child so that he can, in effect, create himself anew. The metamorphosis from child to adult takes about eight or ten years. This volume is concerned only with its beginning, the years from eleven to fourteen, a critical time whose most significant happening is the crisis we call puberty and its aftermath, adolescence.

As every parent knows, no child can fit neatly into someone's stereotype of a particular age group, and least of all, the child growing into adolescence. Nevertheless, this chapter will offer a brief survey of how children in general develop during these years, to provide a rough idea of what to expect and to serve as a general introduction to the rest of the volume.

Growth Toward Puberty

The coming of puberty is heralded about two years before its appearance by a sudden spurt of growth. In girls, the spurt occurs at about ten or eleven, and in boys an average of two years later, although there is a wide variation within the normal range. During a time of relative stability and peace, just when a child had learned how to be a satisfactory child—how to function at home and at school, how to cope with his parents— he is suddenly jolted from within. Perhaps he has been gaining four to five pounds a year. Now a boy will gain thirteen to fourteen pounds and shoot up four to five inches, and a girl will acquire eleven pounds and three to four inches in a year. The growth in height and weight is accompanied by other changes. The girl's breasts begin to bud and then bloom, her hips to widen. She becomes softer and rounder. The boy's shoulders broaden, down grows on his upper lip and chin, and he becomes more muscular and angular. Pubic and underarm hair grows. The voice becomes deeper and fuller. Limbs stretch out faster than the trunk, producing the typical "all arms and legs" appearance. And, of course, the genital organs and the reproductive system begin to develop and soon will be ready to function.

Emotional Pressure

In addition, the glandular functioning has its effect upon his emotions as well as his contours. He becomes moody and restless. He has to be moving, to be on the go. His hands cannot be still. He fiddles with knives and forks and knocks over ketchup bottles, twists his hair while he reads, picks his nose and his nails, cracks his knuckles, worries the hole in the elbow of his sweater, sometimes has a facial tic or other nervous mannerism, and bounces balls off the floor, wall, and ceiling until they resound inside his mother's head. Living with him can be nerve-racking.

Incredibly sensitive, he can pick a fight out of the air. "You made beef stew for supper because you *know* I hate it." Sometimes he seems to be raw to every possibility of hurt. We ask what is the matter and are told, "I don't know; I just feel rotten, that's all." Or, "Can't you leave me alone for once?"

Outbursts of anger may be followed by elation,

crying spells by a spurt of constructive activity; he is enormously resilient. The same child who said on Sunday, "Sure I'll help," retorts on Monday, "Whaddya think I am, your slave or something?" Warm and friendly at times, stubborn, disobedient, and unruly at others, the child of this age can be definitely characterized as unpredictable.

We comment, "Your hair looks lovely pulled back like that."

And she jumps on us, "It does not. It looks awful and you know it."

We suggest, "Wouldn't it be a good idea to do your homework now and play later?"

And he retorts, "Wouldn't it be a good idea to let a person do his own thinking?"

As they approach puberty, children become ever more curious and eager for sexual knowledge, buying *Playboy* magazine like international spies at newsstands far from home and giggling and trading misinformation with friends. A boy is interested in the sensations and size of his penis and anxiously makes comparisons. Girls who have not yet begun to develop find their early-maturing friends drawing away from them toward other interests, and they wonder when it will be their turn. Both sexes are still likely to be uneasy with each other. A boy will tease a girl he likes and be generally unbearable to her. A girl will tend to be aggressive, not very feminine, and perhaps rude to the boys, and she will whisper and giggle about them with her girl friends.

Sooner or later, whether it is wished for or dreaded, puberty arrives. The girl begins to menstruate; the boy becomes capable of ejaculation. The time of this occur-

rence varies considerably. The average age of menarche in girls is about twelve or thirteen, and the average age of first ejaculation in boys is about fifteen, but the normal range extends for several years before and after.

Social Maturation

The difference in social maturation is especially apparent in seventh grade. At parties one can see some boys and girls gyrating sensuously opposite each other to the insistent beat of the music, while others cluster in groups of the same sex and still others play tag, or (boys, mostly) indulge in target practice with peanuts, or play "fountain" with shaken-up bottles of ginger ale. The seventh-grade classroom has little girls in the front row, while squeezed behind their desks in the rear, tall as their mothers and fully blossoming, sit young women of the same age. As a group, the girls tend to tower over the boys in the class at this point and to find most of them babyish and silly.

But the variations are enormous, and development is often uneven. A girl may menstruate and have the contours of a fourteen-year-old and yet behave like an eleven-year-old and cling to the ways of childhood. Or she may behave like a young woman, menstruate, and yet have a preadolescent shape. The various parts of the body grow at different rates of speed, so that at any given time the whole may be out of proportion, disharmonious. That is why youngsters of this age are often awkward, tripping over their own feet, unable to predict the distance between their elbows and lamps and vases. A young person at puberty may fluctuate between childhood and adolescence, sometimes touching both shores within minutes, belonging nowhere, out of step with his own body, and finding no place in his world that truly fits him.

Of course, size and weight, body shape, hairiness, muscularity, breast development, and size of genitals vary not only because of a child's stage of development but also because of his inheritance. Normal variations from the prevailing ideals of femininity and masculinity can make a young person utterly miserable. Frail stature in a boy or a flat chest in a girl—"God just forgot me, that's all," cried one fourteen-year-old—can initiate an all-consuming preoccupation with repairing the "defect." A boy will do push-ups and lift weights every morning and night. A girl will perform breast-developing exercises, followed by daily measurement and the studying of herself in the bathroom mirror—front view, left side, right side. A large nose may lead a child to beg for plastic surgery and set off an endless quest in magazine advertisements for products that will make it appear less noticeable.

Subjective View of Self

The young person's view of himself is, of course, highly subjective. A beautiful girl may focus narrowly on a birthmark on her arm. A homely boy may take enormous pride in his new muscles. A youngster may accept the new odors of his body or find them disgusting, ignore pimples or feel completely blemished by them. Mirrors are indispensable, and the child will search in them endlessly for the secret of who he is and how he looks to others.

A girl may suddenly find the sound of her own

name detestable. Karen is a baby name, Karen is for uglies. Karen wants to know if she can change her name legally—immediately, this afternoon, so that she can inform the teachers tomorrow that they must start calling her—what? It's a problem. How to choose a new name that really embodies her new image? Ah . . . Martha! She rolls it off her tongue, writes it in script, letters it carefully, simply at first and then in ornate letters with a grand "Miss" before it. She plays with her new initials, calls up her best friends and tries "Martha" out on them. Then her little brother gets wind of it and calls after her, "Marthamallow! Marthed potatoes! Martha-partha needs a bartha!" And it's all ruined! She vows to murder him, slams a door in his face—and is back to Karen again.

As the youngster begins to look more grown up, people tend to expect more from him, and often he is not ready for that. He does not know how to behave. He may adopt a kind of protective coloration, an interim disguise, that will mask his vulnerability until he is ready to meet the world as a new person. Eccentric dress, sloppiness and dirtiness, different hair styles and manners of talking or moving—all are ways of covering up as well as trying on new images for size. A pony tail may have been right last month, but the girl must search for the right style to go with her picture of herself today. On the other hand, he may be afraid of making changes, too. We suggest a different frame for his eyeglasses, and he refuses because "everybody is used to seeing me like this."

Exaggeration is one of the keynotes of the stage. The child never just feels good, he feels *marvelous*. He is not blue, he is completely and utterly *miserable*. Her friend Jill has not been a little inconsiderate, she has been *disgusting* and will never be spoken to again.

The French writer Simone de Beauvoir, in *Memories of a Dutiful Daughter*, writes of herself shortly after her first menstrual period:

> I looked awful; my nose was turning red; on my face and the back of my neck there were pimples which I kept picking at nervously. . . . Embarrassed by my body, I developed phobias: for example, I couldn't bear to drink from a glass I had already drunk from. I had nervous tics: I couldn't stop shrugging my shoulder and twitching my nose. "Don't scratch your pimples; don't twitch your nose," my father kept telling me. Not ill-naturedly, but with complete absence of tact, he would pass remarks about my complexion, my acne, my clumsiness which only made my misery worse and aggravated my bad habits. . . . I was hovering . . . between girlhood and womanhood.

New Scope of Understanding

Before he is eleven or twelve, a child's understanding is limited greatly by what he can experience. The concept of burning, for example, is associated with the odor of smoke, the sight of blackened toast, the sensations of a burned finger, the crackle of flames. The idea of justice he can appreciate in terms of being fair, giving everyone his turn, not cheating, getting what is coming to him. But he cannot go much further. Time has to do merely with the clock and when you wake up or go somewhere, and being early or late.

Now, however, he begins to develop a new scope in his intellectual functioning. A qualitative change occurs, which is not just a question of being more intelligent or learning more. He becomes able to reason more logically, to conceptualize, to think abstractly and move from one abstraction to another. He can speculate about the many possible effects of something he wants to do. He can keep a lot of "ifs" in his head at the same time and come down to earth with an answer.

Unfortunately, the pressures of discovering his new self and striving to cope with the changes of puberty often prevent the early adolescent from fully utilizing his burgeoning intellect immediately.

Boys seem to experience urgency about sex sooner than girls and become sexually stimulated by the nearness of a girl or the merest suggestion of a part of the female anatomy. They indulge in fantasies, daydreams, and masturbation as a normal release for this tension. They find an outlet in sports, roughhousing, and other activities for which they have enormous energy. But since their emotional equilibrium is upset, they expend much of their energy just trying to maintain control of themselves. Often this control is shaky; outbursts "for no reason" and other turbulent behavior are common, as well as intense fatigue. The inner demands on their energy may be reflected in seventh- and eighth-grade slumps in schoolwork.

Feeling of Uniqueness

A child will claim that he is not moody, that the rest of the family keeps "bugging" him. If a parent

says, "Don't worry, it's just adolescence," he will bark
back, "It's *not* just adolescence." He is sure that nobody
ever felt this way before. If we say we know how it
feels, that only shows that we don't really understand.
Needing to feel unique, he nevertheless sees no contra-
diction in trying to be like all his friends. They are very
important to him now, and his moods are often precipi-
tated by the breaking of an old relationship or the making of a new one. Because he feels out of step, it helps
to be with others who are going through the same
changes. And, indeed, his main aim is to differentiate
himself from his parents and their generation. The
typically long telephone conversations are part of the
continual dialogues that reassure him that his desires
and feelings are normal.

Before puberty and just afterward, most children
cling to friends of the same sex. Girls often have crushes
on other girls or on female teachers or popular singers
who personify their ideal or have qualities that they admire. They will often affect the mannerisms and style
of such a person, with an eye more for surface detail
than for substance.

Warm and sometimes intense friendships with
young people of the same sex are characteristic. Girls
who see each other every day may exchange letters
several times a week, often addressing them in a flowing
hand that would do justice to a royal calligrapher and
sealing them with wax, for effect and to insure privacy.
These associations help to prepare them for the in-
timacy and gratification of later heterosexual relationships.

Until they are ready, they tend to draw back from

any close attachment to one member of the opposite sex. Wanting love, they nevertheless want to avoid stimulation that they recognize they are not yet up to handling. But in time they become well acquainted with their new bodies and feelings. They come to understand and adapt to the changes, in their parlance, to "put it all together." Girls begin to accept their femininity, to become softer, more receptive to boys; and boys, in their turn, accept their masculinity, yearn to become men.

Self-absorption Is Typical

Growing up, becoming a self-sufficient person with thoughts of one's own, ideas of one's own, values of one's own—an identity—is a slow, gradual process that receives special impetus at the onset of adolescence and does not relent for many years. Parents often feel intense disappointment because it seems that their child has become selfish, and in truth he is now self-absorbed. This need not be a lasting character trait, but simply the normal narcissism of the time. Self-discovery requires a certain amount of introspection and concentration on personal thoughts, feelings, and goals.

Although a child of thirteen or fourteen is still family-centered, still needs his parents' guidance, limits, support, and protection, he is reaching out. He is beginning to feel the need to loosen family ties. He weighs and tests values that he has previously accepted without question. Because his parents' influence is so powerful and their identities are so strong, he must get out from under their shadow if he is to shape himself to his own measure. Often he finds fault, picks fights, rebels, condescends; he can be cruel and hurting. He may sometimes define himself in opposition to his parents. Their ideas are not worth listening to; they don't understand "where it's at" today, how things should be, *anything*. Childlike obedience to parental wishes and standards is simply not conducive to finding out what *he* really thinks, who *he* really is. He wants to walk to his own rhythm.

Yet this pressure to loosen the emotional bond with his parents is often countered in early adolescence by the temptation to solve all his problems by returning home to the warmth and comfort of the nest. Often he is "just like his old self," warm, seeking advice and the old rapport, helpful to sisters or brothers, trying to please, a pleasure to talk to, to have around.

This is a time of life when a child's emotional growth may be slowed if parents look upon his rebellious behavior as a complete repudiation of themselves and everything they have tried to do for him. It is true that some young people do seem to glide through adolescence with enviable grace and a minimum of confusion. Mothers and fathers may point them out as models of comportment who never cause their parents "a moment's worry." The implication seems to be that this period could be tranquil if only one knew the formula. Undoubtedly, adolescence is easier for some youngsters than for others. However, some "easy" adolescents simply have excessively controlling parents who, without realizing it, offer the child less leeway for the normal experimentation of adolescence, show less tolerance for its swings in temperament, its disorder, its challenge. In such households, the young person may not experience the constructive changes that normally occur during this time; his growth toward emotional maturity may be delayed.

Understanding Helps Parent and Child Alike

It does not always do much good to read in a book that a certain period of life produces problems, that parents should accept this as natural and not become upset or alarmed. It is a rare parent who can, at the moment a problem arises, think to herself or himself, "Aha! the terrible two's!" or "So *this* is early adolescence!" But still, if we know fully why children of a certain age behave the way they do, we can sometimes, upon reflection, understand, feel better, and think more clearly how to help them—and ourselves.

Then, too, when we understand that these problems are not evidences of our failures, that our child's rebelliousness and criticisms are necessary to him and not necessarily a reflection of where we have gone wrong as parents and human beings (no matter what the child may say!), we can usually cope better with what comes along.

Parents who understand the pressures on a young person are better able to absorb his provocations without being crushed by them. They can manage not to respond continually with anger or counterpressure, but to provide the support he needs. Gradually, they let go, as he is ready, avoiding a rending power struggle. No amount of intellectual acceptance can prepare parents emotionally for this experience. But as their child becomes a person in his own right, they, too, can become ready to give his season its time.

2

Communicating About Puberty

B**Y THE TIME** our children are eleven or so, most of us have had quite a few conversations with them about how they were born and the physical differences between boys and girls. Probably we have managed better than Sigmund Freud himself, whose son, Martin Freud, recalls in *Man and Father*:

> There had been a discussion in the family about cattle when it had become clear to father that none of his children knew the difference between a bullock and a bull. "You must be told these things," father had exclaimed; but like the majority of fathers, he had done nothing whatever about it.

Probably, we have also prepared our children for the physical changes of puberty, so that they are not left to wonder or be afraid or put together snatches of

misinformation as their bodies begin to mature. Many
parents even today feel that further discussion of sex
and sexuality is not needed until young people are
ready to marry.

This feeling is understandable. Even with society
far more open about sex than it used to be, the topic
still generates powerful emotions, and it is hard to talk
about it with our young. *Seventeen* magazine took note
of parental reluctance in this area recently when it
printed an article by Oscar Rabinowitz with Myron
Brenton explaining to its young readers "How to Talk
to Your Parents About Sex."

Acceptance of Sexuality

But parents need to be aware that their children
are intensely concerned and frequently anxious about
their maturing bodies. They worry about whether they
are developing normally and whether they will be attractive to the opposite sex. We want to give them the
information they need and to reassure them. We want
them to accept the sexual part of themselves as natural
and right and to begin to develop their own values about
sexual behavior.

The appearance of a single pubic hair or the beginning of a curve of the breast may raise questions
in a child's mind. Does this mean that something else
should be happening? Comparison with friends may
reveal wide variations in which part of the body begins
to develop first and how long it takes. The child wonders which is the "right" way and needs to be reassured that the maturing is progressing normally.

A girl may accept her first menstrual period as a

normal occurrence and then be terribly worried because three months pass without another. She needs to know that this is normal, that periods are often not regular during the first year. Slight spotting between periods is normal also, although intermittent bleeding should be discussed with her physician.

A girl's acceptance of the changes in her physique depends greatly upon her feelings about herself as a female. Some girls welcome what is happening with immense satisfaction; others are frightened by what it implies. Some are upset by menstruation; others take it in stride or are proud that they are now able to bear children. The psychiatrist Theodore Lidz says, in *The Person: His Development Through the Life Cycle:*

> During early adolescence, when a girl is learning to feel at home with her woman's body and with woman's role in society, the parents' attitudes are particularly important—their attitudes toward their daughter but also toward one another. When a mother not only accepts her life as a woman but finds fulfillment in it, and when a father admires and appreciates his wife, a girl can welcome the signs that she has become a woman and feel secure that she will be loved and desired as a woman.

The Importance of "Normality"

When a woman gives birth to a child, she wants to know immediately, "Is he normal? Has he got all his fingers and toes, everything he's supposed to have?" Similarly, as our youngsters begin to mature, they worry, "Am I O.K.? Am I attractive? Will boys (or girls) like me?" Breasts have been such an enormous preoccupation in our society, becoming almost synonymous with sex appeal, that it is not surprising that girls with small breasts often fear the boys will not like them. Girls become anxious, too, if one breast grows faster than the other, if they feel they are growing too bosomy, if any hair grows on the breast—indeed, if anything about their faces or bodies seems to them "abnormal" or unattractive.

Boys are generally eager for their shoulders to broaden, their voices to become more manly, and their sexual organs to mature. They will study each other in the showers and lavatories at school to see how they measure up, and they often envy the fellow with the most muscular frame or the largest penis. A boy with a small penis may fear that he will not be man enough for sexual relations. He needs to be told that the size of a penis has no influence on male or female pleasure in intercourse, and also that one cannot judge the size of an erect penis from observing it in its limp state. A smaller penis tends to undergo greater enlargement during erection.

Sometimes a boy becomes alarmed because of a soreness or slight swelling around the nipples. He thinks he may be developing breasts, fears that perhaps he is not "all boy." He needs to be reassured that this is not uncommon in boys his age and usually disappears after a short time.

If a boy or girl continues to be concerned about his anatomy, perhaps he would like to discuss it with a pediatrician, who can make it clear to him that he is normal and answer his questions from a medical view.

Excessive Emphasis on the Physical

With their bodies changing and developing as children grow into adolescence, there is much unavoidable emphasis on physical looks. Young people often come to feel that outward appearances are more important in life than they really are.

The fulfillment of a man or woman in life has very little to do with the size of the breasts or the penis or whether the woman has a pretty face or the man is tall or muscular. It may have a great deal to do with how a man or woman *feels* about his body and himself, whether he feels proud or inferior, lovable or ugly, because this feeling strongly affects the way he expects to be treated and the way he acts toward others. Parents can help a child to feel good about himself, to accept his body and to look forward to what he will become. A parent should not put extra emphasis on the physical by frequent comments about how good-looking or skinny or tall or bosomy a child's friends are. A mother who only asks about a boy's date "Is she pretty?" conveys a value judgment about what she considers important. On the other hand, opportunities abound to illustrate the fact that very good-looking people may be involved in empty marriages and that people who at first glance seem less physically attractive can and do have relationships with wife, husband, children, family, and friends that are warm and loving, supportive and satisfying.

Our efforts should further a youngster's appreciation of himself as he is, not center on experiments to "correct" what we may consider his less attractive features. Such attempts can backfire, as when a mother buys a padded bra for a daughter who had not felt lacking until that moment; or when a girl is reminded continually not to wear her hair pulled back a certain way because "it makes your nose look longer," or urged to choose a certain dress because "it makes you look slimmer." Parents tend to do this more to girls than to boys, but boys are frequently urged to participate more in sports to "put a little muscle on you," or hounded about their eating habits until their few pounds of extra fat or few pimples become far more damaging to their self-esteem than need be.

On the other hand, if a child is obviously concerned about a physical problem, we want to do whatever we can to help him overcome it. Doctors can do more today for acne (see Chapter 7) than when we were adolescent. Medical advice should be sought if the child considers himself too thin or too fat. If a youngster has crooked teeth or another correctable physical problem, a specialist should be consulted. If a family cannot afford the treatment he recommends, perhaps the doctor knows of a clinic where appropriate care can be obtained.

Sometimes a girl feels that having her hair straightened is important, or a boy wants to wear lifts in his shoes. A parent who truly accepts the child as he is and makes this very clear may still decide to go along with such needs at a particular time. We might say, "I think your curly hair looks fine; it's just right for your face. But I can see you hate it, and that's reason enough for us to do something about it right now. I hope that later on you will like your hair as much as we do."

Very often, after an approach like this, a child will

hold off from taking the step. But if she does go ahead, she is less likely to perceive her parent's acquiescence as further proof of her deficiency.

Fathers and Daughters

A father can be particularly helpful to his daughter in this regard. "What! You want to buy cream to cover up your freckles? Why, I fell in love with your mother because of her freckles!" A father's reactions to a daughter are particularly significant now. Dr. Lidz says:

> To a very large degree the girl, despite her careful attention to what she sees in the mirror, and despite her constant comparisons of her own physique with those of her friends and movie starlets, does not achieve an estimate of her charms by what she sees as much as through how she perceives others regard her. The father is very likely to draw away from a daughter entering her teens, feeling that he should no longer be as physically close as previously, and he is often withdrawing from the sexual feelings she induces in him. The daughter often feels that her father now finds her unattractive or is actually repelled by something about her. It requires considerable tact on the part of a father to convey somehow that he considers that his daughter has become attractive and likes the way she looks and yet assume a proper distance.

Boys' Early Sexuality

Some boys become alarmed because they have erections at the slightest sexual stimulus, perhaps just

looking at a particular girl or seeing a sexy picture in a magazine. They may be afraid they are oversexed and might lose control of themselves. Boys become embarrassed, too, by spontaneous erections that occur in nonsexual situations, such as while sitting at a desk studying or riding in a bus. They are convinced that everyone is noticing them, which is not true. The presence of an erection upon awakening, although a universal male experience, may cause anxiety. Boys who understand that these reactions are normal, that they are simply another aspect of becoming an adolescent male and are neither surprising nor shocking to adults, do not need to agonize privately or feel guilty or upset.

Who should talk to a boy about these matters? It is usually the father who talks to his son and the mother who talks to her daughter, but if one parent finds it too difficult (or if it is a one-parent family), the other can often fill in and do a good job if he or she is able to be relaxed and matter-of-fact. Perhaps a parent could confess, "Look, things were different when I was younger, and it's hard for me to talk about this, but I think it's important, so let's try."

Frequently, it is the child who is embarrassed in this situation and not the parents! Adolescent boys and girls can be positively allergic to the slightest mention of their anatomy or sex-related subjects by a mother or a father. If this is true and we feel our youngster might be stewing about something, there are several other possibilities. Books, pamphlets, and articles are impersonal and private and can serve a useful purpose if a child is willing to read one. Sometimes after reading, the child becomes relaxed enough to discuss his con-

cerns with his parents. It is always a good idea to peruse
a book before offering it to a child. No matter how
highly recommended it may be, we should know what
is in it. We may consider the tone too folksy or too
technical for the individual child, or the point of view
may be too "modern" or too old-fashioned for our
home. Some parents prefer to ask their religious counselor to suggest a book that is appropriate for young
people of their faith.

Sex education classes at school can be helpful.
Question-and-answer sessions afterward perform an extra
service in revealing that all the other kids have the same

concerns, even if the questions have been written down and submitted anonymously. If a child has an understanding, intelligent older person he can talk to—an uncle or aunt, a guidance counselor at school, a youth leader at church or community center, or simply a family friend or older brother or sister—that can be enormously helpful. We should make a special effort to utilize such resources fully.

Erotic Dreams

A boy should be prepared well ahead of time for the possibility of having nocturnal emissions. He may already have learned from his friends that "wet dreams" occur, but all sorts of myths abound. He may have been told that they are weakening or that he is losing irreplaceable masculine fluids from his body. He is likely to become embarrassed by the stains on his sheets, not realizing that his parents expect and accept this occurrence. He needs to be told in advance that nocturnal emission is a normal process, that it is the result of sexual excitement caused by dreaming, which reaches a climax with the emission of semen, and that the seminal fluid rapidly replenishes itself.

Such a thoughtful discussion with a child can also deal with the vivid erotic dreams that accompany nocturnal emissions and may occur at other times, and can produce great anxiety. Most of us understand the difference between dreams, fantasies, thoughts, and feelings on the one hand and acts on the other. We can forgive ourselves for having "forbidden" feelings because we are aware that everyone has them. We understand that we are accountable only for what we actually do, not what we think or dream of doing. Being a basically normal person does not mean that one will not have some pretty wild notions sometimes. Young people need to be helped to understand this.

Unbidden Sexual Thoughts

As youngsters are maturing, sexual thoughts come unbidden into their minds and can be as frightening as their dreams and fantasies. A child may imagine having intercourse with a teacher, with his mother, father, brother, or sister. He may imagine being raped or raping someone. He needs to know that others experience these fantasies, and they are nothing to be ashamed of or worry about. They do not mean that he is abnormal or likely to carry out such fantasies.

Homosexual fantasies and dreams are particularly disturbing. Psychologist Wardell B. Pomeroy says:

It is a common experience to be stirred by a sexual feeling toward someone of the same sex through a fantasy, a dream or in some other way. Most people are horrified by such thoughts and feel intensely guilty about having "perverted" feelings. But most of these people will never take part in a homosexual act and those fleeting thoughts will never interfere with their heterosexual lives unless they carry guilt and fear into them.[1]

---

[1] Wardell B. Pomeroy, Ph.D., *Boys and Sex: A Long-needed Modern Sexual Guide for Boys* (New York: Delacorte Press, 1968) p. 72.

What can a parent do to help a child who may be bothered by such fantasies? "If you wait for him to broach the subject himself," warns Dr. Pomeroy, "you will wait forever," because most youngsters would rather admit almost anything than even the most fleeting homosexual thought. Newspaper articles, books, plays, and motion pictures can serve as a springboard for a discussion during which a parent can see that the child understands that his fears are groundless.

Burden of Needless Guilt

A great many adults today were burdened with guilt about childhood feelings and experiences that were, had they but known, common and normal. Today, virtually all physicians and psychiatrists agree, for example, that masturbation is harmless, and most religious groups are reexamining their attitudes on this subject. It is something that most people do in private at one time or another during their lives as a way of releasing sexual tension. The physical effects of masturbation are not significantly different from those of any other sexual activity. Yet, many of our children remain in the dark ages about this form of self-gratification, feeling themselves wicked and dirty and perhaps fearing that they are in some way damaging themselves. Modern parents can spare their youngsters the anguish that earlier generations went through on this account.

Masturbation can become excessive, but so can any other activity. Television-watching, for example, is not bad in itself, but if a child sits glued to the set for hours upon end, one wonders why he cannot find other satisfactions. The problem, then, is not the television-watching but the pressures in his life and the lack of other satisfactions or ways to relieve his tension.

Early Maturers

Young people who begin to mature considerably earlier or later than their peers can have a hard time of it. Eleven-year-old boys who become strongly attracted to girls, while all their friends still hate them, tend to feel out of step and to worry that they must in some way be peculiar. Reluctance to admit a growing attraction to the opposite sex is expressed in a comment by a seventh-grader who had just watched a female classmate saunter by. "If I ever stop hating girls," he remarked to a friend, "she's the one I'll stop hating first!"

But boys who begin to grow tall and mature early usually flex their muscles, admire themselves in the mirror, and feel pleased with themselves.

Girls who shoot up and begin to develop before their classmates are more likely to feel awkward and self-conscious. Of course, some girls are eager to grow up and welcome every sign that they are doing so.

Late Maturers

Late developers seem to suffer more. They feel left behind as, one by one, friends begin to spurt up and have intriguing new interests. A lot of teasing can go on in the locker room, making the child who is slow in maturing feel absolutely miserable. The more physically mature youngsters tend to draw away from the others. Among boys there is talk of "wet dreams," of sex and girls. Among girls there are whispers about boys and romance and love stories. The late starters are apt to feel left out, possibly abnormal, and with a gnawing fear that it may never happen to them.

They need to be reassured, to be told that their time will come. If a mother or father or an admired uncle or aunt has been a late developer, the photograph album can be brought out to illustrate that this runs in the family. Parents should make it clear that every child grows at his own pace. Some grow rapidly and reach their full height as early as thirteen; others begin their growth spurt later but inch up little by little until they may—as with the tortoise and the hare—outstrip the early starters. Each person has a growth rate that is right for him, with wide variations from the "average."

Nevertheless, the late starter may very well feel left out *now*. We might hear, "Why do they keep lining us up by size? I never see grown-ups lined up according to how tall they are," or "Jill has got so stuck-up, she goes around with this bunch of girls who think they're so *big* and spend every Saturday *shopping!*" It is a wrench for parents to see a child in low spirits and not be able to do the one thing the child really wants—speed up the maturation process. But reassuring the boy that he *will* be a man, the girl that she *will* be a woman, that this is one of those things that have to be waited out, may at least relieve their most pressing concern.

It is helpful, too, if a child can become involved in group activities that are not composed only of boys and girls of the same age. A chamber-music group or a chess club, or sewing, woodworking, or typing classes, for example, sometimes include persons of varying ages and take for granted differences in size. Joining such a group affords a good chance, also, to make new friends when some old ones may be drifting away. Also, if a child can, through taking lessons, become proficient in an activity that interests him, it can give a helpful boost to his self-esteem.

Sexual Curiosity

We are likely to find our youngsters again intensely curious about sexual relations, but this time with emphasis on the specific details of intercourse. Although they may have learned what is involved, they cannot quite picture how it happens. As one youngster put it, "Do you just take off all your clothes or what?" Lovemaking and its meaning to a man and woman are a mystery to them. They are more apt to consult each other and whatever books and magazines they can get their hands on—or R-rated motion pictures they can get in to see—than to ask us. And, of course, they imagine much.

One twelve-year-old girl, on a vacation trip with her parents, rushed in to impart the information that two "teen-agers," a boy and a girl, had just checked into the hotel and taken only one room. "I'm sure they're not married . . ." Giggles. "Isn't it against the law? Do you think they have two beds or one in the room?" We are free to gloss over the subject or to try to find out what else she wants to know and help her. Youngsters put out these feelers from time to time as circumstances move them to. If we draw back, they quickly withdraw, too. At this age, they usually do not push for information as they may have done earlier. They are reluctant to admit their ignorance and may be embarrassed about discussing adult sexuality with parents.

We need to pay close attention when children bring themselves to ask questions, because the expressed question often is only part of the child's concern. For example, a girl who has developed early and at thirteen has a woman's breasts, a woman's curves, may ask, "Is it normal for me to grow this much this early?" The mother may respond, "Yes, certainly." But there may be more behind the question. The child may have received stares, remarks about her figure; she may have been noticed by older boys who are responding to her physically. But she herself may be far from ready emotionally for this interest and may be frightened by it. She is not prepared to cope with her new sexual attractiveness, and she needs a chance to express some of her concerns and to be guided and reassured.

There is a wonderful cartoon showing two preteen-age boys coming away from a sex-education lecture, one saying to the other, "I know what they do and I know how they do it—but I don't know *why* they do it." As our youngsters mature, their own physical, glandular, and emotional changes begin to give them an inkling of that "why." And these increased sexual feelings may bother them. They sense that their inner stirrings have something to do with sexual relations, and they may find this frightening or, like the thirteen-year-old just mentioned, feel threatened by possibilities for which they are not yet ready. Some children try to deny the existence of their burgeoning sexuality by clinging to childhood, perhaps refusing to wear more grown-up clothes and avoiding any sort of activity with the opposite sex.

Sometimes parents overlook telling a boy about menstruation and its connection with reproduction or a girl about ejaculation and the changes boys are undergoing. Most women can remember from their adolescent days how some boys seemed to understand immediately why a girl might not feel like swimming on certain days, while others would pester and pester her to go in the water, obviously *ignorant!* It is good for girls and boys to know that the other sex is also undergoing physical changes, with their attendant worries.

The Importance of Early Information

Some parents may be surprised to read in a book that eleven- to fourteen-year-olds should be informed about both contraception and venereal disease. Perhaps we might digress for a moment and tell a true story about a devoted father who took a week's vacation in order to be with his 18-month-old son while his wife was in the hospital giving birth to their second child. The father lovingly ate with his son, played with him, bathed him, and tucked him into bed each night for five days while his wife was away. He never talked to Jess about his mother or even mentioned her name; the boy seemed so happy and preoccupied that it seemed best not to "remind" him that Mommy was missing. Why upset him and raise questions that would be difficult to discuss with a child that young?

This father loved his son enough to give up a week of his vacation time to be with him. He was intelligent enough and aware enough of his child's emotional needs to understand how much a father's presence would mean to Jess while his mother was away. Yet he assumed that the child, who had spent practically every waking hour with his mother for eighteen months, would not even notice that she was missing unless someone else brought up the subject. When Jess's mother returned home, he screamed when she went to pick him up and pushed her away roughly. He refused to let her come near him until evening, when he finally acknowledged her. Whatever thoughts he had had about her absence, one fact emerged clearly: he had noticed it.

Many parents are like that father when it comes to talking to their children about sex-related subjects. They seem to feel that if they don't bring the subjects up, their child will not be concerned with them. They argue that talking about these matters may upset the child, make him overly curious, overstimulate him, or encourage experimentation. In fact, as psychologist Isadore Rubin points out:

> The issue is really not one of ignorance versus information but one of getting information given carefully by responsible sources as opposed to getting it from poorly informed friends or irresponsible sources. Who has not heard stories of young boys who have used plastic wrap as contraceptive, of girls who have douched with soda pop and of others who have taken a few of their mothers' birth control pills? Today, when so many bits of information or misinformation are available in one way or another, it makes sense to provide young persons with a thorough knowledge of contraception in order to counter the dangers of any smattering of

incomplete or incorrect knowledge that they may pick up.

Since not many parents are happy about the idea of their children's having sexual relations at this age, why provide this information *now*? Won't it seem as if we sanction such behavior? Psychiatric thinking, says Dr. Rubin, "suggests that the best time for a child to receive factual information about such subjects is *before* he has reached the age where he must begin to make decisions about it, when his emotions in respect to that information are dormant or less involved.

Sexual Relations

What do we say to an eleven- or twelve-year-old child about birth control? Perhaps something like this (not necessarily all at once in a big speech, but over a period of time in one's own way): "You're not ready to date yet, and there's no hurry. But the time will come when you're going to be dating, falling in love, considering having sexual relations, and you ought to know how we feel about it."

Then, if we feel that sexual fulfillment can be achieved only in a long-term relationship between two people who respect each other and care about each other, we would say so. Or, if it is our belief that sex outside of marriage is wrong, we would tell him that, even though he probably already knows how we feel from things we have said all along. But then we could add, "Our hope is that you will feel as we do about sexual relations, but whatever you decide, we want you to know how to behave responsibly." Children should know the ineffectiveness of homemade improvisations. Young people should understand that there is no reliable "safe" period during the month when a girl cannot conceive. Many parents also see that their daughters have the name of a doctor from whom they can obtain more information if they wish.

An emotionally healthy, sensible young person who has respect for himself is not likely to become promiscuous just because he knows how to prevent pregnancy or is knowledgeable about venereal disease. The young person who engages in irresponsible or self-destructive sexual behavior usually has other, deeper problems, and his sexual activities—or it could be drug-taking or stealing or truancy—are a *symptom* of these difficulties. Knowing how to use contraceptives does not make such a child promiscuous, but it may prevent his behavior from having tragic consequences.

Venereal disease is a major health problem among young people of all social classes in this country today. We need to inform ourselves and our youngsters about it. When we were this age, nobody talked to us about gonorrhea and syphilis because our parents took it for granted that "nice" people did not get such diseases. But, as gynecologist James L. Breen puts it,

Even the nicest person having intercourse with an equally nice person runs the risk of venereal infection and is, therefore, a possible infector of another nice person.

Families need to know the symptoms of venereal disease and that early treatment can bring cure. Many persons are not aware that venereal infection will not disappear without treatment. Thus, because the symptoms often disappear after a time, a person may believe he is cured, whereas the infection is still in his body and later can cause great damage, including sterility, blindness, and death. Books and pamphlets giving detailed information about venereal diseases are available from state and federal departments of health, local health clinics, and many community centers and schools.

Sexual values, of course, go beyond how one feels about the question of premarital intercourse for boys and girls. They involve concern about the other person, an unwillingness to exploit someone else or to hurt someone else (or oneself), or to pressure someone else into a relationship that he does not want or for which he is not emotionally prepared.

Instilling Sexual Values

When we talk to our children about the importance of surrounding a sexual relationship with the deep concern and love of marriage, do they see these values expressed at home? If their parents' relationship is a good one, it will be more difficult for someone to tempt them to accept a sham. Our children are going to make the choices that affect their future, and they may emulate us or they may not. We cannot determine or control their behavior; we can only influence it. And all the indications are that children who are trusted and well informed tend to behave more responsibly.

Our children are living in a society that provides an incredible amount of sexual stimulation—motion pictures, jokes, books, women's clothing, advertising, and so on—and yet frowns on adolescents' being sexually active. We expect them to wait perhaps ten years after they become sexually mature before seeking sexual fulfillment in marriage. Traditionally, daughters have been especially protected, while parents often looked the other way or even smiled approvingly as their sons "sowed their wild oats" with someone else's child. Many husbands and wives today are determined not to make their own children as tense and apprehensive and *warned* as they were.

Complete silence about sex communicates its own message, of course, and leaves our children to the media. One mother was upset to find her fourteen-year-old son reading *The Anderson Tapes*, a detective story heavily spiced with masochistic and sadistic sex. "Most people," she told the boy, "don't need to hurt each other or be hurt in order to enjoy sex." "Oh, I know *that*," he responded impatiently. "I just finished reading *Airport*" (a novel in which all the sex is between married men and women not their wives). Today, inexpensive paperback books, sold at stores where a child buys his ice cream and soda, tell stories of every imaginable kind of sex act. People are writing out their kinkiest sexual fantasies, publishers are printing them, and motion picture companies are filming them. And if our child is not personally exposed to these films or books or magazines—which would be a feat indeed—there is some child at school who is, who sees all, knows all, and tells all, or what he thinks is "all."

If we are not going to pack up and move away from civilization, we must somehow impart to our children healthier ideas about what sex can be.

3

Boy-Girl Relationships

IN SIXTH GRADE, when the children are about eleven, the boy-girl parties usually begin. In some communities this happens a bit earlier, in others a bit later, but the manifestations are the same. While most boys are still inviting their friends to football and baseball and bowling parties and the like, and most girls are giggling with other girls at pajama parties, *some* girls and *some* mothers of girls—and a very few boys—are ready for something else. And the other children in the grade are alerted that something new is beginning.

After a while, as more and more parties are given that include both sexes, more youngsters are drawn into the scene, many reluctantly, not yet ready, joining in the swim only to get a cautious toe wet and then pulling back. Sixth-grade boys are undomesticated creatures, not lending themselves particularly to the social graces. They enjoy the party food, all right, but their elbows knock over glasses of punch onto the furniture and the prized outfits of eleven-year-old girls. In general, they are unsatisfactory party companions. And some of them flatly refuse to put in an appearance at a function where girls are to be present: "Me go to Bill's? Are you kidding? He's having girls!"

A boy will often develop close friendship with another boy at this point, or a group of boys will gang together. Frequently the talk is about sex, but the affection and loyalty are still for a boy's buddies. Boys may ignore girls even though they have begun to be attracted to them, because they need time to get used to these feelings, time to become ready.

Girls also have intense relationships with members of their own sex. Two girls like to be together all the time; they hold hands as they walk along or throw their arms around each other. They call each other on the phone the minute they reach home. They have frequent sleep-over dates and so on. Both boys and girls may find it safer right now to be with members of their own sex. Parents—and children—need not become alarmed if such an attachment has occasional sexual overtones. This is not uncommon around the time of puberty, and youngsters, by and large, eventually move on to interest in the opposite sex. As a matter of fact, such close friendships are absent from the case histories of adult homosexuals. They appear to be a normal step on the way to heterosexual attachments.

Boys and Girls Together

Little by little, boys and girls—some beginning at eleven, others at twelve or thirteen or fourteen or sometimes later—begin to come together for companionship. They see each other in class if they go to a coeducational school. They work and play together at school, in community clubs, and in other activities, and they gab and kid around together at the local "hangouts" where everyone goes for pizza or sandwiches or soda and ice cream. Or they meet "on the block," in the neighborhood. Although interest in each other has heightened and seeing each other matters now, which it didn't a year or two ago, for a while that is all there is to it.

Then, gradually, certain boys and girls may fall into the habit of leaving school together and going for a snack, or perhaps one boy waits for a particular girl. Or maybe they meet every day walking to school or on the bus, and they talk. Or they fall into step after church, or they take music lessons at the same school. There are any number of possibilities. These are not dates, exactly, but the boy and girl are getting to know each other in a casual, comfortable way.

The informality of these early encounters helps youngsters feel more at ease. Nobody has to make conversation for a whole afternoon or evening. There is no set beginning or ending, and the boy does not have the responsibility of "taking out" the girl or of paying her way. This kind of informal meeting can lead to a group of boys and girls going to a movie or the beach or the skating rink, or arranging to meet at a certain point before going on to the football game together. Such casual associations and group activities are healthy learning experiences in boy-girl relationships during which young people find out what members of the opposite sex are like and how to talk to them.

Most youngsters of thirteen or so are not ready for more than that, although, under social pressure, they may decide they are. One mother whose thirteen-year-old daughter asked permission to go on a single date with a boy from school responded, "Do you really want to have to talk to—and listen to—Freddy for one whole evening?" The girl had not thought of it that way at all. "Ugh, no!" she said.

What about these first boy-girl parties? One mother who waited up for her thirteen-year-old son to return home from a party asked him, "What did you do?"

"The same thing they did at parties when you were my age," he told her.

"It was so long ago, I can't remember," his mother persisted.

"Try," he came back—and was out of the room.

Boys in particular have a passion for privacy and an incredible resistance to anything they regard as poking into their affairs. The only way some parents can find out what the kids do at parties is to have one or help chaperone one!

Developing a Social Code

A great deal of trouble and worry in connection with parties can be avoided if parents in a community or the Parent-Teacher Association can get together and agree on a social code. (The Parents League of New York, Inc., at 22 East 60th Street, New York, N.Y. 10022, has published a booklet containing a Suggested Social Code for Teenagers and Their Parents.) In some areas this is natural and easy, but often in big cities, where a child's friends may be drawn from diverse groups, it is difficult. An agreement concerning youngsters in this age range generally includes such points as no parties without at least one parent at home as a chaperone, no drugs or liquor or smoking permitted, and whatever other rules the parents in the community believe are important for their children's well being. In this way, no child or parent is pressured into undesirable situations because "everybody else is doing it," and parents are more able to relax, feeling that other parents will take the same kind of precautions they would. Of course, there are always parents who do not go along, but such an arrangement is still better than just keeping one's fingers crossed.

Some parents feel free to call up the home where a party will be held and ask the host's parents about the arrangements, but this is difficult for many people, and their children usually resent it. Occasionally there is a really considerate mother who calls up each parent whose child is invited to her youngster's party and says, "I just want you to know that my husband and I will be home all evening and that the party will be over at ten."

Good parties for young people of eleven, twelve, and perhaps thirteen need as much planning as parties for very young children, and for much the same reason. The youngsters generate a lot of excitement and energy, and it needs channeling. The boys and girls are not yet ready just to talk to each other or to spend the entire afternoon or evening dancing—or smooching. They will be hungry, and the hostess who wishes to have happy guests is well advised to provide plenty of their favorite foods, keeping in mind that greasy fingers will probably not be wiped on napkins and that olives and pickles are terribly handy to throw. Party activities can be organized in advance by the child, perhaps with a friend or two or perhaps with a parent.

Sometimes parents are less welcoming to their child's friends than they realize. Perhaps the furniture in the living room is "too good." The child just knows that his friends will spill something or knock something over, and that his parents will be annoyed and show it. Or he has to serve fruit punch because his parents are against soda—but all of his friends want soda. Some marvelously secure young people of this age can dare to be different and let the rest of the gang follow along —but not many. Or a parent will treat a boy "like a kid" in front of his friends or embarrass him in other ways. It just becomes easier not to bring anyone home.

When parents are truly hospitable, youngsters may even use their homes as a base for dating. One well-organized young man brought his first date home for lunch; then they went out to play tennis, returned home to change, went off to a television studio to see a show being taped, then back home again to get bicycles for a ride in the park. The date cost him money only for transportation, and he and his girl were too busy to be awkward with each other or to have to depend on conversation for long stretches of time.

Avoiding Social Pressure

Gradually, one's child swings into all this social activity—or he does not. Says Thelma Purtell in *The Intelligent Parents' Guide to Teenagers*:

Strange as it may seem to extroverted fathers and gregarious mothers, there is the occasional child who honestly does not want a social life. These parents suffer much more than their children, feeling that their offspring are afflicted with the agonies they themselves would experience if they were left out of the group. They should realize that there is the possibility that the child is perfectly contented, listening to records, experimenting with chemicals or curled up with a book.

When parents become concerned because their child has not become involved in boy-girl activity, they may begin to exert pressure on him. Sometimes a child is pushed to be more social, to go to a party or participate in another kind of activity. Parents may feel justified if the youngster later says that he had a good time. He may even say he is glad his parents urged him to go. But what is lost if we let a child wait until he himself feels ready? And what is gained when we give a child the feeling that we always know better than he what is good for him? How is he encouraged to develop his own critical faculties, his own judgment about what is best for him to do and how to act in a particular situation? He has to have a sense, as educator John Holt says in *What Do I Do Monday?*, "of being in charge of his life." He has to know that if he were in charge it would not necessarily turn out badly.

Many young people are avid for boy-girl activities at an early age. They are precocious, or eager to get a head start, or simply curious to see what all the talk is about. For such youngsters, parents sometimes need to revise their ideas about how early to permit certain activities if a child is truly ready.

The First Dance

Do you remember your first dance? Many people, particularly women, do. And many bear deep scars from that night and other first boy-girl encounters. A woman recalls:

I had been hoping and hoping this one boy would ask me to the school dance. He was the only fellow in the grade taller than I was, and we had been sitting in the back of the classroom next to each other for two years. He did ask me, finally, and I remember that my mother and I had a big hassle over lipstick and whether I should wear my glasses —I was blind without them, but I hated them. And then the boy ditched me the minute we got there! He spent the entire evening with a short, cute girl named Dolores who was wearing a crimson dress with a skirt that flared when she danced. None of the other boys came near me. I felt like a big lump. I managed to get through the evening making trips between the food table and the record table and the ladies' room, trying hard not to look at *them*. After that miserable night nobody could convince me it was "lovely to be so nice and tall," and I walked hunched over for years.

And a thirteen-year-old girl of the 1970's told it all in one short sentence when she arrived home after her *second* dance. "Oh, mommy," she exclaimed, beaming, "I wasn't a wallflower tonight!"

Boys need not worry that nobody will ask them to dance, but they are nervous, too. They are afraid they won't know what to do or will do something dumb and embarrass themselves. And it would be humiliating if they asked a girl to dance and she said no. "I guess I took a lot of time checking it all out, you know, seeing who was there and all," said one young blade of thirteen, rather coolly, after his first dance. "There was a lot of good stuff to eat, too. . . . Did I dance with anyone? Well, not exactly."

Of course, if a boy is turned down, he can work up his courage and ask another girl to dance. He does not have to put in waiting time. So dances are, in the end, not the potential torture for boys that they are for girls. A lot of this can be avoided if the youngsters can be won over to an afternoon or evening of some party games and some dancing, with planned, relaxed ways to help them come together with a partner—from catching a balloon with a partner's name in it to choosing a pair of shoes from a pile and searching, Cinderella-style, for their owner.

Helping a Child Belong

It is hard to know who suffers more, the child who is having social trouble, feels shy, ugly, left out, painfully self-conscious, or her parents. Most youngsters want very much to belong. The suffering of adolescents drawing toward their first encounters with the opposite sex is often real and deep, and its impact may affect the person's thinking and feeling for a long time.

How can we help a child move more easily in the social world? We need to know first what his trouble is, why he is having difficulty. It is vital to try to look at the problem through the child's eyes. A lovely young person may, for some reason, consider herself unattractive and be extremely self-conscious because of this. Her problem is not her looks, but how she feels about them.

Sometimes when a child does not begin to date or go to school dances or parties, it is the parent and not the child who begins to get frantic (although the child catches the parent's mood soon enough). Parents may try berating a child into sociability—if you didn't slouch, act so bossy, look so sloppy, twiddle your hair, or wherever the problem is pinned, you would get along better. A child who is already humiliated by her wallflower status at dances may be told, "You just stand there; you don't even try." Sometimes these admonitions help; often not. But even if they help, the cost may be too high in terms of what it does to the child to achieve his measure of success.

Overemphasis on Popularity

Some parents put a destructive emphasis on popularity, implying or even saying outright, if you do this, you'll be popular; or, if you behave that way, you'll never be popular. A child can come to feel that the be-all and end-all is popularity, rather than the true development of his own personality and individuality, his identity. How much of himself will he betray in the fevered search for a multitude of friends, preferably, perhaps, of a socially desirable type? Would he prefer not to talk so much, smile so much? Is it more natural for him to be a more private person? The tragedy in this kind of betrayal of self is that it attracts friends who are drawn toward his disguise, forcing him to con-

tinue in it, while the kind of youngsters to whom he is naturally inclined turn elsewhere for friends.

Sometimes a child lacks confidence because his parents are too hard on him in one way or another. Perhaps they have too-high standards, are rarely satisfied with his performance or his friends or his activities. With the child who lacks self-confidence, we should ease up as much as we can. If a child has a rather serious personality difficulty—is often unkind, rude, sarcastic to his contemporaries, has many fears, feels that others make fun of him, or has some other problem that interferes with his relationships with the children in school and in the neighborhood—we need to know what is causing his feelings and his behavior.

Some children are simply late bloomers. They make their way slowly and blossom in their own good time at fifteen or even at seventeen. What they need from us is confidence and support—and patience—until they are ready to come into their own.

Some girls—and boys—will never shine at the big dance, never be relaxed at parties, but they do just fine when they are with girls and boys working at a school activity or sharing any mutual interest. We should encourage this type of child to become involved in the kinds of activities that are her strong point and help her to avoid dances and other affairs that become situations of humiliation and misery and may indeed convince her that she is inferior or "unpopular."

Build on the Child's Assets

What are her assets? Can she play an instrument, cook, sew, garden or grow house plants from seed, swim, type, repair things, paint, sculpt, play chess, collect stamps or coins, take marvelous pictures; is she a crackerjack skater or tennis player, or does she love to watch baseball or football? The list is endless. A youngster can be helped to develop her interests and skills. Then she will tend naturally to get to know others who are similarly inclined. Of course, the interest must be genuine. Young people themselves always advise against phoniness. As one girl put it, "It's no good pretending she likes something she doesn't; she won't have any fun. So what's the good of it?"

A young person who is interested in others will often find that they return the interest. But it is hard for anyone, child or adult, to care about others if he is unhappy and has a low opinion of himself. Here again, we need to know why he feels that way in order to help him.

Social poise at a party, the ability to make light chit-chat, to fit in and be part of a gay crowd, come easy to only a fortunate few. Most young people are awkward in social situations until they have had enough experience and success to help them develop confidence. They may be so anxious that they clam up; they may want so badly to be interesting that they cannot think of anything to say.

A youngster will envy those children who seem to "have it all together"—who seem, at an early age, to know who they are, where they are going, and how to handle themselves with both boys and girls. These lucky ones just don't seem to have the same worries he has, he thinks. A child knows that *he* tries to hide his uncertainty, but he often fails to realize that many others shiver under their poise, that bragging is usually an attempt to cover up feelings of inferiority, that a great many young people his age are actually in the same boat he is, just—only just—pushing off from shore.

Sometimes it helps to explain that early success does not necessarily mean that a young person will always be ahead. What charms the girls at thirteen, for example, may bore them at sixteen; and a thirteen-year-old boy's idea of feminine charm will probably change and develop as he gets older. But this kind of philosophizing may not help much, partly because the young people do not really believe it and partly because it is this minute that is important anyway.

Striking a Balance

If young people can be supported through these early occasions, they will probably begin to take hold themselves as time goes on. Parents need to strike a balance between sharing their knowledge and overwhelming the child with advice and suggestions. Some parents have a knack for passing on their social know-how, giving a child a needed hint in a constructive way that he can accept. Others only make a child more self-conscious and angry at what he construes as criticism.

Youngsters can be cliquish and cruel, and the child who is left out may suffer deeply. Contrary to popular myth, such suffering rarely ennobles. When a child begins to feel himself or herself a failure at social encounters, he becomes even more self-conscious and uneasy. The problem compounds itself. Then others tend to find him or her more difficult to be with, and it becomes harder and harder to break the cycle. Whatever can be done to help is worth it. Sometimes a parent can chaperone frequent excursions to the skating rink, the bowling alley, the public pool, or wherever the young people in the community like to go. Gathering together our child and a few other young people for an afternoon's fun is an excellent way to encourage wholesome relationships with others—if our child likes the idea. It offers a youngster a chance to get to know and be known by others his own age, to gain experience talking, learn how to be a good listener, empathize with others' thoughts, hopes, joys, sorrows, pains.

The First Date

When they begin to date, both boys and girls should understand that the other sex worries, too, about how they look and what to say and do. A boy may be attracted to a girl but afraid of her at the same time; she may laugh at him or not take him seriously. A girl worries that he may find her dull or uninteresting or may talk about her with his friends. Neither one has ever thought about it before, but what do girls (boys) like to talk about? He has not given much thought to manners before, either, but now he is hesitant—will he know how to do the "right" thing at the right time? He has a moment of panic when he notices his dirty fingernails and remembers how many times his mother warned him that girls find this revolting; he wonders what else about him may be revolting.

Girls worry that they will not be asked out; boys are anxious that they may be turned down—the same kind of situation that prevailed at the dances and will continue, more or less, for a while. If a boy is rejected by a girl, we can try to help him see her "No, thank you" in its proper perspective and not feel diminished by it.

He needs to understand that he is not crazy about every girl he meets, nice though many of them may be, so he cannot expect that every girl will want to be with him. If he is turned down, perhaps it is because she is too shy, or her mother is very protective, or she only likes brunettes—none of which ought to affect his self-esteem, disappointing though it may be. Of course, the same thing goes for girls. Our aim should be not to prevent all hurt, which is not possible, but to try to see that the hurts of today do not really injure the child's opinion of himself and that he learns from them as much as he can.

We should get across to our children how inevitable and natural it is to make mistakes at the beginning, to say the wrong thing to a girl, to offend a boy in some way, to be so nervous that one forgets a name and so cannot make an expected introduction—the possibilities for humiliation are infinite. Parents have to try to help youngsters recognize that self-consciousness is par for the course and that the best cure for it is to be considerate of the person one is with.

Boy-Girl Behavior Differences

Boys and girls also should be made aware of a basic difference between them that affects their behavior. Even though changes occur in girls' bodies at puberty as they do in boys', most girls do not suddenly become interested in sex as the average boy does. Girls are interested in boys in a new way, but it is more in terms of dating and romance than in sexual relations. Says Eric W. Johnson in *How to Live Through Junior High School:*

> The early adolescent sexual feelings of boys are commonly satisfied not by contacts with girls, but by private activities: nocturnal emissions and, much more frequently, masturbation. But while this male sexual activity is going on, many boys are socially very anti-girl, whereas the girls, although not erotically aroused, are socially greatly interested in association with the other sex.

When dating does begin, girls may flirt and act enticingly without realizing that they are exciting boys sexually. They may be genuinely surprised at the boys' reactions. A boy may think that this is his fault, that he has made a mistake. But the problem arises because of the difference in outlook between boys and girls at this point. It is possible, however, that if the double standard disappears and women and men become equally free *and equally responsible* sexually, we will find that girls experience stronger sexual pressure at an earlier age.

If at the start a child is frequently rebuffed in his or her desire for dates, he may want to retreat for a while.

We may wish he would not "give up." We may want to talk about it in an effort to help, but he may not want to think about it, much less talk with us about it. And he probably does not think of himself as "giving up" but merely as sitting out the situation for the present. The average child will test the water again after a time. Meanwhile, his wishes should be respected. If other things are going well at school and at home, and if he has some social contact with boys and girls in clubs or other activities, there should be no pressure on him to do anything more. Of course, if a child has no friends or is unhappy for a long period of time, help is obviously needed.

Is the Child Ready for Dating?

Perhaps he is not really ready for dating. He is not yet grown up enough, and it was actually group or parental pressure, not his own wishes, that impelled him toward dating. It has been observed that mothers tend to be content when boys take time to be interested in dating but are more apt to press a girl to test her wings. One of the most important things we can do for a child this age is to help him cope with pressures to begin dating before he is ready and to support him in moving toward it at his own pace. Being ready to date implies a certain maturity, a desire to spend time with someone of the opposite sex, being secure and relaxed enough and skilled enough socially to go on a single date without its being more strain than pleasure. Young people are better off if they do not push themselves or feel pushed by their parents. They can learn to get along with the opposite sex in various other social settings.

We need to judge a child's readiness; we should not be influenced by the fact that his peers are dating, or by the child's insistence if we sense that he really is not ready. Some children are ready at an earlier age than others. Physical development is not the only guide.

A young person may be intensely curious about the other sex but not interested in actually dating for a while. We may push a child into dating before he is ready by giving him the feeling that we expect it or consider it desirable.

We can help our child and ourselves by giving some thought to how we really feel about his dating. One mother confessed that she felt somewhat depressed when her son went on his first date. She is not unusual —or sick. A young person's dating presages the time when someone else will be as close to him as we are now, when he will be ready to leave home and start a family of his own. If we recognize such feelings in ourselves, we are better able to prevent them from affecting our behavior with our child and his friends. Unrecognized feelings like this give rise to situations in which a daughter can never find a boy whom her father considers "good enough" for her, or a mother is critical of every girl her son takes out.

Masculine and Feminine Roles

We do have, and need to accept responsibility for, a strong influence on the way our children feel about femininity and masculinity. The way a husband and wife treat each other and the way they feel about themselves is part of the everyday experience of their children's lives. Is a mother admiring of her husband; does she respect his judgment and his decisions? Does she enjoy being a wife and mother? Or is she hostile, cold, competitive? Is she submissive, domineering, or an equal? Does she like being a woman? Is she affectionate and loving? Both sons and daughters receive daily doses

of her prescription of what men and women are and ought to be and how they stand in relation to each other. Similar influence is exerted by their father's behavior. What does he think of women, of his wife? Does he treat her with warmth, kindness, consideration? Or is he insensitive or sarcastic or indifferent?

What does masculine mean in our society? Traditionally, we think of strength, of dominance, of a defender of the home. What does feminine mean? Traditionally soft, submissive, gentle, nurturant. But not everyone agrees any more what little girls are made of, and what they ought to be doing with their lives. It seems certain that women will have more choice in the future; more possibilities will be open to them and more arrangements available to them to continue their careers after their children are born if that is what they want. And more girls will be seeking husbands who are willing to accept a new kind of equality in marriage. A magazine article published recently told of a contractual agreement between a young man and his wife to take equal responsibility for all the jobs in the household, child care included. Under this arrangement, each can pursue his career equally. The wife does not have to feel that she can work only if she can juggle the job, children, cooking, and cleaning. Some men are deciding that they, too, have been cheated by the traditional division of labor in the home. They want to see more of their children and are willing for their wives to help them support the family.

Today's youth seem to be blurring the distinction between masculinity and femininity in their dress, appearance, and interests. Perhaps certain things should have no gender. In the past, girls have been brought up to love ballet, boys to care about baseball. Boys were given the idea that music and art were somehow girlish, and girls that these were suitable feminine pursuits. Then boys and girls married and often complained that they did not have common interests. No one—least of all women—has ever denied that gentleness and tenderness are important in a husband and father; but it was rarely listed under the qualities labeled male, and many men in our society have felt they had to be tender on the sly so as not to be caught at it. Surely boys ought to be able to cry and girls to climb trees without being thought of as, respectively, sissies and tomboys. What is left of being a man or a woman if these cultural attitudes are changed? Only physical differences? Maybe not. Maybe we are moving not toward a unisex, but toward new definitions of the masculine and feminine roles. These roles have been differently defined in other cultures, and in other eras, so that they need not be considered sacrosanct.

Of course, many men—and women—are uncomfortable about the idea of more freedom for women and prefer the traditional outlook. The important point for parents is that whatever our own inclinations, it is clear that times are changing, and we should not assume limitations on women that may not exist for our daughters. And perhaps we ought to prepare our sons for new kinds of relationships, in which it is not necessarily assumed that women will submerge their interests to those of their husbands.

Helping the Child Perceive His Role

The way a father behaves toward his daughter influences the way she thinks about herself and her femaleness. If a father shows that he feels his daughter is developing well, is lovely, this gives her confidence in herself. Does she have to prove herself to win his approval, or does he value her for what she is? Is he loving or cold? Whatever kind of man he is, he is her first and most important model of what men are and should be. His treatment of her conditions her expectations for the future.

A daughter is also helped immeasurably by a close relationship with a mother who accepts herself as a woman, who is emotionally available as needed, who can delight in all her daughter's strengths without becoming competitive, and who knows how to cherish a budding rose, thorns and all.

Similarly, a son needs the feeling that he is his father's idea of what a boy should be, that his father respects him as a fellow male. Does he feel that his father cares about him, is interested in him, and is proud of how he is maturing? All of this is conveyed in actions as well as, sometimes more than, in words. A father who says he is pleased with his son's woodworking or bowling score, for example, but finds fault with him continually as they work or play, negates his words. A father who is considerate and supportive of his son gives his boy the feeling that he is a worthwhile person. Is the father authoritative but flexible, firm but reasonable? Can he be gentle as well as strong? This is going to be the son's deepest image of what a man should be.

In a home where there is no father, a mother needs to be careful not to lean too much on her son, particularly as he is maturing. A son should be treated as a son, not expected to take a man's place in the home. Wherever possible, other men should be brought into his life. Can he often visit or be visited by an uncle or grandfather or a close family friend? Some mothers engage a "boy-sitter" one afternoon a week when their children are small, but a boy this age begins to outgrow such an arrangement. Sometimes it is possible to have a live-in male student who functions as a kind of big brother to a boy. This can become complicated, however, if there is a teen-age daughter in the home as well. When a mother takes her son on trips, it is good if another boy can go along as well. Each family will fashion its own ways of meeting the problem. But a boy needs masculine figures in his life, should not grow up in too feminine a world.

What kind of mother does a boy want and need? "A motherly one," said one boy. But motherly means different things at different ages. Right now, it means being somewhat less protective than before and neither domineering nor too permissive. As with father and daughter, a mother who shows her son that she has pride in his ability and accomplishments and confidence in him, treats him with warmth, affection, and respect, helps him to become a man.

The influence upon children of their parents' marriage cannot be overestimated. Do parents appreciate each other and respect each other? This strongly influences the child's feelings about relationships between men and women. If parents have frequent bitter quarrels, this can cause young people more anguish than is always understood. Unfortunately, however, a great many homes are not as happy as both partners would wish. Although they may be resigned to their relationship or working to improve it, both need to help their children get along in the situation as it exists. Such parents can try not to let the bitterness of the marital situation spill over into hostility toward the children. It is important, too, to guard against letting a child fill the emotional place of a husband or wife. Where it is humanly possible, parents should try not to let the children witness or overhear marital discord. Beyond that, and as the children grow older, ways might be found to show them that not all marriages are like this and that relationships between men and women can be close and good.

4
The Struggle
Over
Limits

Twelve-year-old ron woke up Monday morning
feeling exhausted and not much like getting out of
bed. "Why did you let me watch that movie until
11:30?" he berated his mother. "You knew I'd be tired
in the morning!" Needless to say, Ron had insisted the
night before that he would be just fine in the morning,
that he was quite old enough to decide for himself how
much sleep he needed. He had pressured his mother
until she finally gave in, more from fatigue than con-
viction.

Now, this morning, he is telling her in effect that
she is supposed to be the responsible one, that she has
no right to let him do anything he wants. What he
means, really, is that he is counting on his parents to
provide wise and firm limits for him. How else, after all,
can he safely push? And push he must, because he is
on the final lap of his journey toward independence.
Unfortunately, there is a time lag between his desire to

be on his own and his ability to control his impulses and regulate himself. And deep down he knows it. This is where his parents come in. They must be able to say "No" to him even when he pleads or fights, and to say "Yes" even when they are still fearful, to let him go when they still want to hold him safely and warmly to them.

Perhaps the most difficult thing we must do as parents is to help our children become independent of us. We nurture them from the day of their birth, we guide them through difficult times, we comfort them when they are miserable, and we share their delights and their triumphs. We are part of all the days of their lives. All this time we are deriving the deepest satisfaction from giving of ourselves, from the feeling of being important to our children, of being needed, necessary to their very existence.

The Beginning of Independence

Then a time comes in their lives—adolescence—whose natural end is their independence of us. Their freedom. It is difficult to face because, for one thing, we cannot really envision what kind of relationship we will have with our children when they, too, are adults. So we know only what we are losing—our children as children. The irony is that the better we have done our job, the more independent of us they will truly be. Still, independence can mean many things.

Do you remember how exhausted and uncertain you felt during your first weeks at home with your new baby? How the continual round of feeding and diapering and responding to cries made you fear that you might never again have a moment to yourself?

One harried new mother phoned her pediatrician after a particularly wearing night spent more by the crib than in bed. "When will he become less demanding?" she implored.

"Never!" responded the doctor. What he neglected to mention, of course, was that her baby would be demanding in a very different way at four months than he was at four weeks and than he would be at four years. And that the mother, who would gain in knowledge and experience, might well find subsequent demands upon her easier to bear, and surely more interesting, than the current strain upon her weary body.

Just so, in our relationship with our grown children, independence need not mean emotional separation. Strong bonds of warmth and love can coexist with independence. The situation between our children and us will change, but if things go well, we can look forward to many years of being part of each other's lives in a way that all of us will find rewarding.

Letting Our Children Go

How do we move toward this time? How do we let go? Not in a burst at sixteen or eighteen or twenty-one, but gradually, little by little as the children push in this direction or that and we bend and give and hold back, often not knowing if we have let them go too far or held on too tight.

And our children do not make things any easier for us. In order to find themselves, they must begin to separate themselves from us; indeed, they must push us away. In early adolescence they do this with a vengeance, all the while holding on for dear life because they are not yet ready to stand alone. The thirteen-year-old daughter who presses to go out on a date with a boy may be terrified if we actually permit it. She will feel unloved unless we restrict her actions to protect her from venturing beyond her depth.

In order to become free of us, they must attack our way of doing things. In order to find out what they think, they must challenge our thinking. Like the writer who said, "How do I know what I think until I see what I write," our children often seem to say, "How can I know what I *don't* think until I hear what *you* say."

Sometimes parents are so controlling that they insist that children accept their way under all circumstances. On the beach one hot summer day, a mother pressed her daughter, "Wear your sandals until you reach the water, or you'll burn your feet." The girl, who was at least thirteen, resisted: "If the sand burns my feet, I'll come back and get my sandals." But her mother continued to press, unable to permit the child, even in this very limited instance, the experience of finding out for herself, of possibly getting burned.

How much toleration do we have for our children's experimentation? It is not easy to watch a child set out in the wrong direction and not call out "Stop!" When our children were small, we would stop them if we thought they might be risking a broken leg, but we would tend to stand aside if the worst possibility was only a bad scrape. This is the kind of thinking we have to update to meet today's problems. Needless to say, they are far more sophisticated, but our basic dilemma is the same. Overprotection may give parents peace of mind and extend their control, but it is not in the best interests of the child. Suzanne Strait Fremon writes, in *Children and Their Parents Toward Maturity:*

> A child who is too protected will never develop his sense of danger, his judgment of people, his evaluation of circumstances, his knowledge of his own possibilities and limitations, and his ability to organize himself and his actions.

We try to protect our children from all kinds of things while gradually letting them take over. Again, that is very much the trick of being a parent, sensing when they are ready to take over and neither hovering too long nor not long enough.

Freedom to Come and Go

By the time a child reaches eleven, he has already spread his wings in the neighborhood. He goes to school alone, he can travel on the bus and go to the grocery store, the shoe repairer, and the bakery if they are fairly near. The schedule, of course, varies depending on the community. Where public transportation is available, he can usually go to his piano lesson alone, or to have his braces adjusted or his hair cut. But now he begins to want to venture farther afield, to go to a movie or concert alone or with friends, to go rowing in the park, to go to an amusement park on the other side of town, to come home alone from a friend's house at night. How can we tell when he is ready?

Very much as we have been doing all along—by

knowing our own child. How capable is he really? How much self-confidence does he have? Does he tend to be cautious or reckless? How comfortable is he with people? In case of emergency, would he go to someone for help? How does he react when he is frightened? Does he panic, or would he think clearly enough to call home? What are the realistic dangers in a particular situation; for example, if a hundred twelve-year-old boys were to go off to that amusement park, what might happen to one or all of them? We have to balance the dangers of children not experiencing freedom enough for healthy growth with the dangers of their being frightened or hurt. If we are too permissive, a child can get into serious difficulty because of lack of experience, or he may feel that we don't care.

Sometimes we have to say "No." Even though he sounds and looks as though we are forbidding him what he wants most in the whole world, we decide that the responsibility is too much for him just yet. Occasionally a child who is very much afraid of something will push for it as a way of denying his fear to himself. But a child should not have to be so brave or so daring in a situation that has real dangers.

We must judge each request on its individual merits. Perhaps he asks to go on an all-day outing to the beach with some friends. We say we feel this is too dangerous for him this year. He replies that he is quite capable of looking out for himself; why can't we have faith in him? Although he is pressing hard—we never want him to have any fun, we spoil everything, and so on—we sense that underneath he is nervous about the whole idea. He very much needs us to say "No" and to help him get out of the situation gracefully without losing face with his friends.

When he has cooled off, we can discuss with him trips to places he might enjoy that are not quite so far afield and would help him gain experience and confidence. We can talk about next year or the year after and try to help him understand that we will let him go when we think he is ready. He may angrily reject this faraway possibility now, but he will begin to look toward it and it will help—the door is not closed forever.

We may feel more comfortable with a child who admits fear, who says, for example, "I'd like to go on the train alone to visit Grandma, but I'm a little nervous about it." With him, we can discuss the pros and cons, decide when to encourage and when to hold back, learn how he feels about various experiences. A child who will not admit he is frightened, who boasts with bravado, "Of course I can do it," is generally harder to help.

The Need for Guidance

A youngster develops over the years a sense of his environment, where it is sensible to go and where it is not. He learns to answer such questions as: Should I come home from there by myself after dark? Is that a good place for a girl to go alone? Would I get into trouble there? But meanwhile we need to guide him.

We need not go along with the crowd. We have the responsibility to protect our child, and we cannot delegate it to those generous and devil-may-care parents all his friends seem to have. But it is true that the only child who cannot—when it happens too often—does become stigmatized, left out. So we need to balance his need to be part of his group against the importance in our eyes of a particular restriction.

In order to justify their restrictions, parents may be tempted to exaggerate the dangers in a situation. But we cannot expect a child to trust what we tell him about heroin, for example, if we have lied to him all along about other things. If he wants to come home alone at night from a party, we can talk over with him the real possibilities of danger. Then, even if he does not come around entirely to our view, we expect him to comply with our wishes. We should not feel that we have to frighten him in order to get him to obey. If there is an honest relationship between parents and child, the child will respect the parents and be more apt to be swayed by their opinions. Remember that, as times goes on, he will increasingly tend to make his own decisions, with or without our counsel. His trust in us is important to both of us.

Some parents hesitate to take a strong position lest they be considered dictatorial or punitive, or alienate their youngster. They mistake a child's rebelliousness and criticisms as evidence of their failure or of the child's lack of respect and love for them. It is very hard to feel otherwise. We know that beefing is par for the course—a kind of background music to adolescence—but each confrontation hits us afresh. It is *our* child criticizing *us*. It really is hard to feel sure of ourselves and secure in our opinions. Think of it sometimes as if he and we were playing parts in a play. His role is to push us, and our role is to stand firm. If we were

to give in, to change our role, it would throw everything off—most of all him.

The Child's Room

Not only do we limit our child's freedom outside
the home, but also inside it. And nowhere are our rules
more apt to be questioned or ignored than in the area
of his room. "This is MY room. These are MY belongings. Why can't I live in a mess if that's what I like?"
If some social scientist made a study, he would probably find that every ten minutes, at least, somewhere in
the United States, a twelve-year-old girl was saying this
to her mother. Most of us these days find it rather
difficult to come back with, "Cleanliness is next to
godliness." All right then, why *does* her room have to
be in order?

Are we saying to ourself that banana peels on the
floor, muddy shoes on the bedspread are unhealthy, un-
safe, and revolting? No doubt we can reasonably look
upon decaying fruit skins and things of that ilk as
hazardous, but the bedspread is not that clear-cut, particularly if it can be thrown into the washing machine
once a week (possibly by her) and needs no ironing.
And revolting? To whom?

Well, we cannot believe that she can work well
amid that junkheap. She is not learning good habits
and will gradually descend into sloth, there perhaps to
remain. But most of us know capable adults who work
well, thrive even, in comparable disorganization. Of
course, it does seem as if a person could work more
efficiently if she did not have to spend time looking
for objects long since buried under other objects. But

some children seem to possess built-in divining rods: they know exactly where under that mountain lies that red ballpoint pen.

At this point we may have to face the fact that we want her room in order because *we* just cannot stand living with that mess. Could we keep her door closed all day and pretend we have one less room in the house? No? It still drives us crazy?

Presumably by the time our child is eleven or twelve we have taught her everything we know about organizing belongings and placing soiled clothes in the laundry hamper, so what we are dealing with here is not a failure of intellect on her part. Still, we could offer to devote some time to helping her arrange her things, and it is possible that she does not have enough shelf space or whatever. But the chances are, quite frankly, that her room is messy because she likes it that way.

Rethinking the Problem

We will want to think carefully about how much rearrangement of her surroundings we feel justified in demanding. How much cleanliness and neatness do we have in mind, and how often would we expect her to put her room into that condition? She is right in considering her room a special preserve, a part of her, really. At the moment it reflects her feelings, for reasons that we—and possibly she—cannot fathom. She is comfortable with it this way. So it is not a good idea to push her any further than is absolutely necessary. Would a once-a-week, or when-company-is-coming, pick-up and put-away be enough if she agrees to make her bed and empty her wastebasket every day and not

leave food or drink lying around indiscriminately? Would we be able to agree to close our eyes to the clutter at other times?

We can discuss our feelings and ideas with our child. We can try to limit ourself in time and space— that is, to this room and the present; try not to torture ourself with visions of our daughter as a wife and mother with cockroaches in the cupboard and potato chips crackling underfoot, all because she never learned (and we failed to teach her) to keep her room clean. She still has some growing up to do, so it is not sensible for us to think of her or label her as a slob for life.

Most of us feel we have to convince our children that clean is better than dirty, that order is more esthetically pleasing than mess. We want them to *care* whether their rooms are neat or not. This caring may come in time or it may not, but it must come from within the child.

When children share a room and one likes order and the other likes clutter, it is sometimes possible to divide the room so that each has an area to live in as she likes. We may hang a movable curtain, or install a sliding, accordion-pleated room divider. In any case, each child must agree to respect the other's private domain and know who is responsible for doing what cleaning and when. The more clear-cut and understood that can be, the better.

How He Looks

The way a child dresses, the way he combs his hair, the way he arranges himself, is also of deep importance to him. Whether he is sloppy or neat, whether he looks like every one of his friends or has his own particular style, it is what he wants for himself. Parents need to encourage cleanliness and to offer guidance about dress and grooming, but it is a sensitive area. If a boy's hair is always standing up in back, his father might invite him in for a conversation one Saturday morning while he is shaving and then casually offer him some of his hair cream while he is using it. If a girl wears her hair in an unflattering way, a mother might point out hairdos in a magazine that she thinks would look well on her daughter.

The trouble, though, is that this sort of hinting often turns into pushing, or the manner in which a suggestion is made belittles the way the child is now. We don't want our child to become dissatisfied with his appearance or more self-conscious. He cannot accept our guidance if he sees it as a put-down of his taste, or of him. Wherever possible, we should permit him to reject our advice and do things his way. Youngsters of this age tend to be sloppy. Sometimes they wish they could throw a big blanket over those disturbing bodies of theirs. Some of them do! Dirtiness seems to be more fashionable than ever among some children today, but most of us are still unhappy and embarrassed by a sloppy, dirty child. Some days it may seem that all we talk about is his appearance. We decide that his messy habits are ruining our relationship.

How much can we bear? We must bear what we can, keep reminding ourself that he will probably outgrow this phase sooner or later. Sooner, if we can avoid making it an issue, making him feel that his rights and his manhood are at stake. If we look around, we will notice that many of his friends also look as if their parents had neither bathtub nor mirror. It is important also not to comment upon his appearance in front of other people.

When we are exasperated because he cannot seem to wash—in fact, he smells—it is not helpful to call him a slob or a pig. We can remember how we feel when he calls us selfish or a mean mother. It happens to most parents, and yet it can make us feel awful—and angry, too. And it does not particularly make us feel like doing what he wants. It is this way with our children, also. The worst thing about a label like slob or stupid or lazy is that after a while a child gets to believe it himself. Most of us know a grown woman who seems to be always on the go and yet refers to herself as lazy.

It is good sometimes to think back to our own adolescence, to the ways our own parents enforced limits that helped us to learn and grow. Memories of being embarrassed in front of friends or members of the family, or of being made to feel incompetent or hopeless, are also useful. They can help us to understand how our children feel if we do this to them.

Often it helps with a child to agree to a kind of performance contract. Together we discuss the various points at issue. We consider his ideas; he considers ours. We come up with a compromise that we are both willing to live with. Neither of us may be completely satisfied, and yet it seems a way of meeting our mutual needs. This does not imply total equality between parent and child, nor does it mean that we are giving up our parental authority. We remain free to exercise control as necessary. But when a child is able to participate in regulating himself, he moves closer to self-control, which is the ultimate aim of all discipline.

The Telephone

Unfortunately, the telephone problem is going to get worse before it gets better. Children this age need to talk on the phone. What they do, really, is to have extended visits with one another this way, relieved of the anxiety and inhibitions that often accompany face-to-face talks. They gossip, they chatter, they giggle, they whisper. They discuss in endless detail all the happenings of the day they have just lived through. They make dates and break dates. They compare homework. They call to remind one another to watch a television show or to bring colored pencils to school tomorrow or to wear their matching purple jeans. They recount in excruciating detail the movie they saw last Saturday. They make loving noises and hating noises, ecstatic noises and revolting noises. Sometimes they eat while they talk, or listen to records, or even do exercises. They talk lying down or standing up or in any one of a variety of contorted positions on a chair, a bed, or the floor. They complain about their parents, their teachers, their brothers and sisters, their other friends. The telephone for them is an escape from the family, a release from tension, a tool for developing social skills, a joy. They can talk on it for a very, very long time.

Needless to say, there is nothing inherently harmful in all this, and they never seem to get sore throats from it. Unfortunately for them, other people in the household want to be able to make and receive calls. If the family can afford a second phone during these years, the situation does become easier. But if not, we can try setting a firm time limit on calls and a firm limit on the number of calls per day or per week. In addition to the inconvenience, youngsters this age can often run up astronomical phone bills. When this money is needed elsewhere in the family budget, a definite limit on the number of calls per child must be set for financial reasons. This means that every call above the agreed-upon number must be paid for out of the child's own money; we can hang a checklist and collection box on the wall next to the phone, if necessary.

Sometimes, however, phone bills upset parents who would not object to the same money being spent on other, equally nonessential, activities. It is a way of looking at things. Such a parent might feel guilty calling a dear friend in another town once in a while and running up a two-dollar phone bill. But she would feel perfectly comfortable spending that sum on round-trip bus fare to visit the friend, or spending even more to have lunch with her at a restaurant. If we have this difficulty, we might want to reconsider our attitude toward telephone bills in view of the genuine importance of the telephone to an adolescent.

Verbal Hostility

We have to be willing to accept a certain amount of outspoken resentment and hostility from our youngsters. The child has to test himself, his opinions and values, against us. He should not have to deny his feelings or hide them; he cannot learn to handle them that way. But at the same time, he is greatly in need of our continuing support. In the past, parents often felt it was wrong, disloyal, for children to express anger or hatred toward them. Children were made to feel guilty for those feelings. But today we know that our children cannot feel love for us all the time, that it is normal for them to feel positively murderous toward us some of the time. These feelings, if we accept them philosophically, do not last, and they do not damage the good basic relationship we have with our children.

This does not mean that we have to tolerate continual verbal abuse. The child has a right to complain, but not endlessly. Neither does he want us to lecture him continually. He is entitled to bring up the subject again for review, but not every minute or at any hour of the day or night. He cannot throw things, use language that offends us, or become more abusive than we can bear.

Remember, too, that he does not have to agree with our restrictions; he just has to abide by them. It is not helpful to keep at him in an effort to prove that we are right and he is wrong. This causes a great deal of wear and tear on both of us and gets nowhere. He has to do it, but he does not have to like it.

We must not expect our son to feel warmly toward us when he has to come home earlier than he wanted, or our daughter to be gracious every night when she is clearing the table. Remember that this is a stage of life when a child may become annoyed with us even when we think we are being lovely. One mother tells of exclaiming "Oh, how cute you look!" when her twelve-year-old daughter appeared in a new pants outfit one morning. To which the girl replied rudely, "If everyone's going to be saying that to me all day, I might as well go right in and take it off!"

Setting Bedtime

When we say, "You must be in bed by 9:30," is this because our child happens to need ten hours of sleep each night, or because we think children of twelve should have a 9:30 bedtime, or because we need the peace and quiet and privacy? It is helpful to know the "why" of the rules when our child protests: "Nobody in the whole class has to be in bed as early as I do!" "I'm not tired. Why do I have to go to bed?" "I'm old enough to decide how late I should stay up."

Some children seem able to regulate themselves at a fairly early age. They wash when they are dirty, they do their homework before it piles up, and they actually go to sleep when they are sleepy. If a girl like this stays up late one night reading or watching television or gabbing on the phone with a friend, she will probably decide on her own to get to bed early the next night. If we regulate this child's bedtime arbitrarily or fuss on the rare evenings when she stays up too late, we are interfering with her growth. She is learning more when the natural consequences of her actions continue to influence her: she stays up late, she is sleepy the next day, she goes to bed early that night. The other way—she stays up late, mother is grumpy—may get her to bed at a set time for as long as she lives at home, but it is not helpful to her in the long run.

What about the child who knows he is exhausted when he stays up beyond a certain time but just cannot seem to take that fact into account when he is involved in a hot game of gin rummy with his brother? He needs us to control him for a while yet. Bedtime is at 9:30 (or whenever); he can gripe, he can plead, but bedtime is at 9:30. We are not angry with him, because we know that nobody likes to have to go to bed when they are enjoying themselves, and we are not asking him to be delighted. We are only asking him to do what experience has shown is best for him. Exceptions? "I have just this one more chapter of *Tom Sawyer* to read" or ". . . just these three more math problems to do." If this is a regular nightly story, we need to be firm. We might suggest that he set his alarm for an hour earlier and finish the next morning if he absolutely must. Some youngsters work better this way. On the other hand, if he is usually willing to abide by the rules, we will want to make an exception from time to time, making clear that it *is* an exception.

Changing the Rules

Perhaps "everybody" really is allowed to stay up later than he is. He feels like a baby with so early a bedtime. He is ashamed when his friends call at 9:45 and are told that he is in bed. Or he lacks the time to get his work done and have some fun, too. Maybe we need to renegotiate the contract. What bedtime would he feel was sensible? What does he do with his time? Is he so loaded with schoolwork and chores and practicing the trumpet that he honestly has no time to take it easy? Does he play around a lot after he comes home from school? Every child needs a chance to unwind after the school day, but perhaps he could be starting the things he has to do a little earlier? Is there anything he would give up that could provide him with more time for the things he feels he is missing? How much sleep does he actually need each night in order to function well? Would we be willing to experiment for a week with a bedtime an hour later and see how he feels? It is a good idea, when we have agreed to something like this, to let the week go by without day-to-day comments such as, "You look a little sleepy this morning," or "You had the extra time and I see you still didn't get your closet cleaned out." We should make it a fair chance, meaning that both of us have an opportunity to evaluate how it is working without bias. If we have a complaint about his closet or something else he is supposed to do, it is worth talking to him about these things separately and not letting our feelings about them complicate the bedtime arrangements.

As a youngster becomes able to get along with less sleep, his staying up late may infringe upon his parents' leisure, their time to relax and talk alone together. It is tempting, then, to insist upon an unreasonably early bedtime. And since we feel a little guilty about pushing him to bed just to get him out of the way, we are apt to camouflage our needs with talk about "his own good." The issue of bedtime then gets cluttered up with odds and ends—our guilt, his anger —that really need not be there and that just add unnecessary complications.

Why should we feel guilty about wanting a little relaxation? Our needs are legitimate. But why should he go to bed just because we do not want him around? When the situation is reexamined as a problem in logistics, it often can be worked out reasonably well. If he has a room of his own or there is a family room, he could be asked to retire to it after a certain time, without boisterous play or clamorous comings and goings. If children share a room and one goes to sleep earlier than the other, space needs to be found for the older one to work or enjoy himself without disturbing us. Will the kitchen do? Some arrangement can be worked out if a family puts their heads together. If there is one thing that adolescent children recognize, it is the need for privacy. If they feel welcome to come and go as they choose most of the time, they are likely to accept restrictions that ensure everyone's rights after a certain hour in the evening.

On the other hand, some children do feel like second-class citizens living in their parents' home. Perhaps they are constantly asked to remove themselves and their belongings from the place where their parents are together. Or perhaps their parents express their demands in such a way as to reinforce that feeling: "As long as you're living in *my* house you must . . ." wipe your feet or be polite or whatever. It is much better to place the emphasis on mutual respect and concern for the feelings and needs of everyone in the household. After all, we really want our children to think of it as their home, too. And often we will want to balance our need for adult conversation (or quiet!) with their need to feel part of the family group, one of us.

Household Chores

Sometimes a mother hesitates to insist that children help with household chores lest she be considered unkind or unreasonable. She may feel, for example, that her children should help her after dinner. But they have made it clear that they have their own work to do and think it is unfair that they should have to help with hers. So she does not press, but she is angry each night as everyone gets up and leaves her to clean up after them. In one way or another, her children will feel her resentment, and it is not good for them or for her.

When a child's help is needed, he should be expected to give it—and sometimes to beef about it. But certain things can be done to make it more palatable.

We should not expect a perfect job. We probably will not get it, and he will dread helping if he can never do the job well enough to suit us.

We should try not to wait until we must have the milk immediately before asking him to go to the store. If he has some leeway in choosing when to perform a particular task, he is more likely to perform it graciously.

We should not interrupt his homework to ask him to do a job. His work deserves to be respected also.

It is not undermining his sense of responsibility if we give him a day off occasionally. It is good for him to feel that when he is overtired, or overburdened with work, or feeling low, someone cares and makes allowances.

We know that life is easier for us because he helps. We know that it is nicer for us in the kitchen when he is setting the table or peeling the potatoes while we put the roast on. Let him know it, too. "Well, you finally remembered to put the salt and pepper on the table" is not praise!

Needless to say, it is better to give him a job he

likes than one he hates. Few grown-ups rush to do jobs they dislike.

When two children dislike working alone, can they get along well enough to share jobs?

When he comes in to help with a chip on his shoulder, we should try to overlook it. He is thinking, "Okay, I'll help, but don't expect me to be nice about it." This is a compromise of sorts; we are getting the help; he is getting the satisfaction of showing how he feels. That's fair enough.

Do household jobs teach a child responsibility? It is hard to say. Surely the child whose job it is to feed the dog or the turtle—and who remembers to do it on his own—feels important and necessary to the animal. Then again, if he is always forgetting and feeling guilty about that, or his mother is always reminding him or doing it for him, it is another matter. Most household chores that children are asked to do, such as folding laundry, helping with the dishes, and the like, are deadly dull. In themselves they give a child no feeling of achievement at all. He has to do his share because he is told to. But satisfaction will come only from feeling that he has been important to us. Unfortunately, a job is often robbed of this by our constant criticism of a child's performance or our grumpiness because he is late in doing it. Or his work is discredited by our own general feeling of contempt for housework. Where any of these conditions prevail, a youngster will get little that is positive out of doing his assigned task.

When a child is downright miserable at having to do a certain chore and does it poorly or ungraciously or both, there is no way we can be sincerely appreciative.

It is a good idea under such circumstances to offer him the chance to help in some other way, if possible.

Sometimes it is infuriating to read about being reasonable with our children. We feel like the six-year-old who, when urged to be good, retorted "My good is all run out." For one reason or another we just could not cope all day; when the children misbehaved we charged through the house creating havoc; we screamed at our daughter, exploded at our son. The way we feel now, what we need is a new son, a new daughter, and a new disposition. But we can take heart. It really is impossible to be kind and understanding and reasonable all the time. If we forgive ourself, we will find ourself better able to forgive the children, too.

There may be periods when it seems to a child that a rule holds him back every time he tries to turn around. He will tell us he feels "fenced in." He will fight hard on a tiny matter that we know cannot be that important to him. He will complain that he "can't breathe around here." Sometimes life in general becomes too much for a youngster. He lets down on compliance, and we, understandably, tighten up. But this is the very moment he can stand it least. Then, too, a parent sometimes presses too hard, making too many rules or getting after a child without giving him a chance to follow through on his own, in his own way. Or a child outgrows some of the restrictions that were suitable last year, or only last month. They feel as tight on him as last year's clothes.

If we sense that our child is feeling particularly pressured, we can let up on him for a while and give him the extra breathing space he needs. Leeway given

in the right spirit at the right time is just as important
as proper limits.

Television Privileges

Joe's mother came home one day from a P-TA
meeting and informed her son, "You said that nobody
else in your class has to finish his homework before he
can watch TV, but Mrs. Schultz told me that Teddy
isn't allowed to watch TV on school nights at all!"

When Joe returned from school the next afternoon
he told his mother the actual situation. "You're right
about the rules at Teddy's house, Mom," he said. "But
the thing is, his mother is always going out evenings
and Teddy cheats."

We all like to feel that our children will follow our
rules whether we are there or not. We take a dim view
of "cheating," of complying only when someone is there
to see. But there are ways in which parents make such
rebellion more likely. Is Teddy's mother inviting defeat
by asking too much? Teddy sees his parents go out
to enjoy themselves after their working day. If he has
done his work, perhaps he thinks he should be able to
enjoy himself as well.

Joe, on the other hand, wants to watch a program
or two before he settles down to work. Would he do
his work conscientiously afterward and would he leave
himself sufficient time? If his parents insist that he
finish his homework first, will he rush through it in
order to get to the TV set? Work before play is a good
habit to develop, but it can be overdone. A child often
needs to unwind after school. Television provides for
some youngsters this age a release from all the cares of

the school day or from new and disturbing sexual impulses.

When a child seems to be living in front of the television set to the exclusion of practically everything else, parents would want to find out why—is he bored, unhappy, having trouble with school, friends—and to attempt to deal with the underlying problem.

If parents do decide to limit TV watching, or anything else, they should know why they are restricting their child and what they expect to accomplish by it. Are they restricting TV, for example, because they feel the youngster should be playing outdoors more, or spending time with friends, or reading, or studying, or helping about the house? Or do they disapprove of the programs he chooses to watch?

Perhaps his interest or activity could be stimulated

in another area. A positive desire to do something else, perhaps with a parent, would draw him away from TV and be less apt to leave him feeling deprived. It is wise to ask the child how much television he thinks is a fair amount per week. Parents sometimes overlook this step, expecting that the child will make outrageous demands that would only cause more conflict. But when children are approached this way, they generally try to be responsible. Sometimes a child asks for the chance to cut down on his own, rather than have a set ration of hours per day or week imposed on him by his parents. This is worth giving a try.

In a large family, squabbling over who watches what may be reduced if everyone joins in preparing a weekly schedule for watching. Sometimes a father insists upon watching "the game" whenever it is on, or a mother feels that a movie she wants to see deserves priority over a child's regular shows for the evening. Or a child may feel that because he watches a certain show every Tuesday at 7:30 he owns that time slot. The resolving of this kind of conflict depends on the values of the family. In some families it is expected that the hard-working wage-earner deserves priority over the rest of the family, or that the parents do because they are the parents. In others everyone takes a hand in deciding what programs are watched.

The way in which parents announce their preferences to their children is important. There is a world of difference between, "Tonight's game is the playoff, sure to be a great one. I know you'll enjoy it; why don't you watch it with me?" and "I'm watching the game, and that's that!" Still more difficult for a child is, "If you were considerate you'd appreciate how tired I am when I come home from a day's work; you'd want me to watch my show" or "If you had any taste, you wouldn't be watching that junk anyway." When parents make decisions unilaterally, they have to be ready to take the beefing. Attempts to avoid this by making the child feel guilty or witless are unfair, hard for a youngster to handle, and not conducive to good parent-child relationships in the long run.

Limits for Our Sake

Along the same line, there are some things in a family that children should be expected to do, or refrain from doing, for their parents' comfort or peace of mind. There is nothing inherently wrong, for example, with a youngster's listening for hours on end to what a parent considers perfectly dreadful music. But he ought to be willing to turn off or lower the hi-fi when another minute of that particular record will drive the parent up the wall.

Some parents find it difficult to make a request like this without camouflaging it. Instead of asking the child to stop the music because they need to have quiet for a while, they feel that they have to have a "real" reason. So they criticize the music. An argument then ensues about the music, the child's taste, and/or the child's rights as a human being to like what he likes and play what he likes to play. All of this can be avoided simply by asking the child for a kindness. When there is give and take in a family, parents often do things they don't feel like doing because the child needs or wants them. A child will, too, if the request does not imply criticism and he can comply with dignity.

When They Break the Rules

We make certain rules, we are clear on them, the children are clear on them (more or less), but compliance is spotty. One day he comes home on time; the next day he forgets. He is chronically late to school. The phone bill will break the bank. What do we do?

Child psychiatrist Fritz Redl writes, in *Pre-Adolescents: What Makes Them Tick*, that most of the more serious difficulties between children and parents could be avoided. They are not inherent in the actual problems of growth. They are produced by the way in which adults react to them. He does not advocate that parents give up and let children do as they wish. What he suggests is that parents study each situation as it arises and decide what to allow and where to draw the line, or intervene. Inherent in his thinking is that parents need to try to be as flexible as they can, to tolerate rebelliousness within certain limits, during these difficult years. We do want our youngsters to become self-disciplined, to develop "inner controls," but this is not necessarily synonymous with getting them to do what we want them to do.

But suppose limits are being consistently overstepped and our patience is wearing thin? Let us pose an extreme situation. Our child walks in one day and tells us he has robbed a bank. Would we yell at him, punish him? Chances are, our first thought would be what in the world has got into him. In other words, why? Similarly, when a child cannot seem to get to school on time, we need to determine why. Is it because he is afraid of a tough kid on the bus, or is having difficulty with the work, or the other children, or the teacher? Or is he (even at this age) reluctant to leave us? These various possibilities leave us with different avenues of approach to the same behavior. Dr. Redl suggests, "Don't fight the behavior. Interpret the cause of it first, then judge how much and in what way you should interfere." If a child is having serious trouble in school, for example, we won't want to make an issue of his tardiness, but to work with the problem that is causing it.

Reasons Behind the Rules

We must consider, too, just how wholehearted we are about what we ask of our child. Sometimes a parent actually encourages a child's misbehavior without realizing it, because the parent derives subtle satisfaction from it. For example, a father looks at his daughter gabbing away to yet another friend on the telephone and says, "If you're not on the phone with one kid, it's another. Don't they know anyone else's number?" No doubt he is genuinely annoyed that every time he wants to make a call, there is his daughter tying up the line. But deep down, this rather shy man is pleased by his daughter's popularity, and his manner of criticizing her communicates this to her. He is telling her to cut down her use of the phone, but on a deeper level he is really encouraging her to do just the opposite.

Take another situation. An eleven-year-old boy constantly tracks mud into the house from the ballfield and never seems able to wash all the dirt from his face and hands. His mother is always telling him to wipe his feet before entering the house, to use a washcloth and soap, and so on. But something deep inside the impeccably neat woman delights in this muddy-faced ball player of hers, and that feeling is communicated to the child. It is not something that he could put into words, but something he senses. So all the while she thinks that he is disobeying her (and so does he!), he is actually responding to what she really desires. If we are not getting compliance from a child, we should give some thoughts to whether it is what we honestly want.

Possibility of Compromise

When there has been a good deal of argument and resistance about an issue, we might try a hands-off policy, no nagging or even hinting for, say, a week. Then, if our child has not made an effort to do better on his own, we can have a talk with him to see how he thinks he could improve his performance or why he feels he cannot. Perhaps he leaves his bed unmade every day when it is supposed to be made before he leaves for school. He says, "I can't help it, Mom. It's the one job around here I just can't stand!" Perhaps he could make an arrangement with his sister, who hates taking her turn at clearing the table. Or perhaps there is something he could do for us in return for our making his bed. Or maybe if he leaves his door closed every day we could decide it was not that important and give in on this issue. If discussion yields no meeting of minds, and we feel it is time to insist, we should state our decision without rancor, tell him what we will expect from him in the future, and then change the subject.

If he still does not comply, we may need to restrict privileges or exert pressure in some other fair way (a child this age is too old for spanking). But we must be ready to ease up as soon as he shows a willingness to comply. Parents who constantly meet rebellion with angry threats and punishments succeed either in thoroughly cowing a child or simply fostering more rebellion, often concealed—a child is less and less at home, for example.

As time goes on, we will be able to supervise less and less of our youngster's life. Mutual respect and affection will be all we have going for us, our only credit in the bank, as it were. We want the kind of relationship that will enhance our influence on him later in all kinds of situations when he is away from us, affect his decisions about how fast he drives a car, what he does about sex, alcohol, cigarettes, or experimenting with drugs.

The child always needs to know why he must do this or may not do that. This is more than ever true as he gets older. It is hard to explain the reason for every little thing we ask, but in general a youngster should understand the reasons behind the rules that regulate his life. He should have a chance to discuss all restrictions with us and to have his thoughts and feelings respected. When we have to overrule him, we will want to do so in a manner that preserves his self-respect. Although they beef, children by and large accept reasonable rules. They need rules. Rules, when they allow adequate room for growth, provide the security that enables a youngster to test and develop his powers in an emotionally healthy fashion.

5

Values

NEWSPAPERS CARRY HEADLINES such as: "Mayor Indicted on Three Counts of Fraud"; "Plot to Fix Criminal Cases Laid to County Prosecutor"; President Accused of Lying to the People." And we must try to give our children acceptable values by which to live. The task gets harder all the time. How can we help our young people to lead worthwhile lives in a society that often does not support their best instincts?

The truth is that nobody really knows precisely how values are passed on from one generation to another. We need to be somewhat suspicious of anyone who says: "This is how to produce a good person." In ancient times Socrates pointed out the many noble Greek leaders who had unworthy sons. We can all find among our acquaintances examples of fine people whose children are no credit to them—or the reverse, children who have become admirable human beings despite rather unprincipled parents.

Virtue, therefore, is not necessarily contagious. A parent who is generous, honest, just, and responsible is not guaranteed children with the same assortment of commendable qualities. Good example is not always sufficient. What is more, children perceive their parents differently from the way the rest of the world does. They see another side of us. For example, a mother who gives generously of her time to the hospital-fund drive may be stingy with her time at home.

Deciding Our Standards

Then, too, how certain are we of the standards we want to impart to our children? A group of New York City parents met one evening to discuss values. They explored such questions as, "Do our children reflect in their actions the way they are treated by their parents? Is it wrong to be manipulative in planning for our children? Do a child's friends have greater influence on him today than they did in the past? Would we honestly be willing to allow our children to live lives that are significantly different from ours, with different values from our own? If today's children are more flagrant in their rebellion against authority, is it because they are more open, more truthful, or more bold? If we as parents do not agree on absolutes, how can our children develop standards?" The group attempted to agree on a single value that all thought was necessary and could not do so. Today social change is rapid. Good people do not all agree on what is most important.

Are we ready for our children to judge us by our own standards? Sometimes parents are not. After all, when our children were younger, they accepted pretty much everything we told them about life, and they believed our judgments about people. Now they are beginning to question our views and to be critical of our behavior. It is healthy, but hard to take. Perhaps we find ourselves saying things like "You think you know better?" or "What makes you the expert all of a sudden?" Yesterday we were ten feet tall, but their eyes reflect a smaller image now.

In order to find their own identity, our children must develop their own values, seek out new experiences, and make their own judgments about them. They will try on for size new attitudes and new behavior, accepting this, rejecting that. Erik Erikson writes, in *Childhood and Society:*

> The adolescent mind is essentially a mind of the moratorium . . . between the morality learned by the child and the ethics to be developed by the adult.

Does that mean we ought to forget about trying to impart to our children the most important thing about ourselves, our values? That it is just a question of potluck what they pick up from us and others? Our common sense tells us this is not true, either. We know as well as we know anything that something of what we are as human beings comes across to our children. We also know that a child is naturally more receptive to his parents' values if he feels they value him. In other words, our relationship with our child will affect what he will accept and make part of himself in the course of developing his own ethic.

Differences in Background

Most of us want our children to work through to their own values—just as long as they end up where we are! This is not as unfair as it may sound. If we are thoughtful people who think seriously about our values, it is natural to want to share our perspective with our children. But how can they think just as we do? We are a generation older. Our experience of life is both greater and different. Some parents, for example, have struggled up from an impoverished background and become able to give their families a way of life and luxuries unknown to them when they were children. Toys, clothes, surroundings that were the parents' childhood dream are their children's birthright. But can these children have the same feelings about work, about money, about possessions that their parents have? If you fly to the top of a mountain by helicopter, can you feel the same about the view from the summit as those who hiked uphill all day to reach it? The values we have developed through our experience of life will not necessarily have the same meaning to someone without that experience.

We often hear of parents who struggle to put their children through college only to have the youngsters drop out before graduation. These young people seem not to value all the hard work and sacrifice that went into earning the money for their education. Why? In some cases it is relevant to ask what value was actually conveyed to the child by the parents' struggle. What else was sacrificed along the way? Did the struggle become more important than the child himself? Sometimes a father takes a second job in order to put aside money for a child's future schooling and because of this is rarely home, often tired and irritable. Perhaps that youngster would benefit more from the presence of a father who is nice to be with and can spend more time at home. But it is hard to know what is best to do.

There are no easy answers. It is not wrong to work hard so that children will have more than their parents had. But when children are used to fulfill their parents' own youthful dreams, they may rebel, needing to make their own choices.

Our example *is* a powerful force in educating our children. How do we measure up to what we expect of them? Do we tend to have one set of rules of behavior for our children and another for our friends? Do we ask them to value what we do not? Are we, for example, as polite to them and their friends as we expect them to be to us and other adults? Do we do as we please with our own leisure time but harp at them to use their free time profitably? We teach our children early not to make cutting comments about people in their presence. We don't say, "Mommy, why is that lady so fat?" or "Why does that man have such a funny nose?" while the person is within hearing. But many parents feel free to criticize their children's friends about their appearance: "When are you going to cut your hair?" or "Don't you ever comb it?" or "What kind of getup is that?" Young people are easily hurt. They may hide their hurt behind bravado or even rudeness, but they are vulnerable.

Imparting Our Values

How does a child learn to be honest, to care about others, to be courageous, just, and generous? Given an opportunity to see the answers to a test, what makes one child cheat and another not? What makes one child join the crowd in picking on a weakling and another stand up for the underdog?

Partly it has to do with the way *we* handle ourselves and the people in our lives, the daily ethical judgments *we* make about one thing or another. Our youngsters draw conclusions about our values as they see us practice them. Small children take it for granted that parents will have more privileges than they and can do all kinds of things they tell the kids not to do. But at this age, youngsters begin to inspect parental behavior very closely and to point out mercilessly any discrepancy between what we do and what we expect of them. They also notice how parents treat each other and their own parents.

Some young people feel that their mother and father are fairly happy and lead productive lives. Others perceive spiritual emptiness, loneliness, unhappiness, lack of concern for others. When we think about imparting values to our children, we need to take a careful look at ourselves and ponder what our children can see in us that they will want to emulate.

We all have our weaknesses. Often it is easier for us to detect wrongdoing in another than to face up to it in ourselves. Recently a mother found after a long railroad trip that the conductor had failed to punch about $30 worth of tickets. She was about to cash them in when it occurred to her that this would amount to stealing. Just the week before she had roundly condemned a friend of her son's when she heard he had taken a model plane kit from a local store. Now she had been about to indulge in something she realized was comparable. All of us may not be quite so reflective, but we find that when our youngsters reach this age they develop an annoying habit of noticing this sort of thing, of doing our reflecting for us. When this happens, we can try to rationalize our behavior. Or we can admit our shortcoming and try to change.

Values Are Changing

That parents could preach one set of values to their children and live by another was possibly more acceptable to youth when we were growing up. Certainly, a discrepancy between what people claim to value and what they practice in their lives has never been unusual. Psychologist Kenneth Keniston says in a lecture, "Youth and Violence: The Contexts of Moral Crisis":

When social change is slow and institutions are powerful and unchanging, there occurs what we might term the "institutionalism of hypocrisy." Children and adolescents routinely learn when it is "reasonable" to expect that the values people profess will be implemented in their behavior and when it is not reasonable. . . . In almost all societies, a "sincere" man who "honestly" believes one set of values is frequently allowed to ignore them completely, for example, in the practice of his business, in many interpersonal relationships . . . in relationships to his children, and so on—all because these areas have been officially defined as exempt from the application of his credal values.

But today values seem to be changing so quickly that "exemptions from them have not yet been defined and the universal gap between principle and practice appears in all its nakedness." This contributes, says Keniston, "to one of the central characteristics of postmodern youth: they insist on taking seriously a great variety of political, personal and social principles which 'no one in his right mind' ever before thought of attempting to extend to dealings with strangers, relations between races or international politics. . . . They frequently come from highly principled families with whose principles they continue to agree; and they have the outrageous temerity to insist that individuals and societies live by the values they preach."

A more compassionate view of this problem is taken by psychiatrist Stanley Lesser, who believes that parents want their children to see an image of themselves as they would like to be, their ideal self. He says, as quoted by Morton Hunt in an article entitled "The Gentle Art of Understanding Your Parents":

And children want to see their parents as exemplifying that ideal. In adolescence, however, children become even more aware of reality; they interpret the difference between ideal and reality as hypocrisy or duplicity, and become deeply disillusioned. After some years, however, most children realize that what they saw was neither hypocrisy nor duplicity but only the normal gap between one's aims and one's achievements; with this realization, they achieve an adult relationship with their parents. The pity is that so many years are wasted before understanding overcomes disillusionment and replaces it with compassion and deepened love.

Conflicting Principles

It is difficult to live by our high principles. When the clerk at the supermarket makes a mistake in our favor, most of us accept it quietly, rationalizing that this makes up for one of the many times we are sure the clerk has overcharged us. This kind of negotiating with principle allows us to do what we want instead of what we should do. So shame is another reason for hypocrisy, shame that we are not better than we are. We would like to be better and, quite naturally, try some of the time to convince others that we are what we wish we were.

How can we help our children to be better than we are? They, like us, must develop their own moral judgment. Professor Lawrence Kohlberg of Harvard University suggests that one way to help children toward this goal is to form the habit of discussing situations that require moral reasoning. He believes that so-called character-building programs that teach youngsters *rules* of behavior—always be generous, loyal, honest, and so on—do not lead to real moral growth unless the reasoning behind the rules eventually is accepted by the individual. In a lecture, "Education for Justice: A Modern Statement of the Platonic View," he defines moral education as "the asking of questions and the pointing of the way, not the giving of answers, the leading of men upward, not the putting into the mind of knowledge that was not there before."

In a series of experiments, Kohlberg and his associates exposed children to situations in which a moral conflict existed and there was no simple right or wrong answer. For example, they asked, "Before the Civil War, we had laws that allowed slavery. According to the law, if a slave escaped, he had to be returned to his owner like a runaway horse. Some people who didn't believe in slavery disobeyed the law and hid the runaway slaves and helped them to escape. Were they doing right or wrong?" The psychologists drew the children into discussions by asking them further questions as they responded. They found that after a while, with this kind of "practice," children's comprehension of moral situations increased and their moral judgment became more mature. They also found that children usually preferred the highest level of moral reasoning they could understand. Their sense of justice was sharpened.

Talking Out Right and Wrong

Situations in the child's life can be used as springboards for discussion. Our son comes home with this story: He was playing ball with some friends in the park, and despite their polite requests a man walked right across the field, interrupting the game. One of the players, in anger, threw the ball at the man's legs. The man picked up the ball and refused to return it, although it did not belong to the boy who had thrown it and this was going to stop the game for all the other boys. Our son feels strongly that this man had no right to do as he did, but he realizes that the boy who threw the ball was wrong, too. One might get into such questions as: If you do someone an injury, are they justified in getting back at you any way they can, or are there limits? Children can be helped to become more sensitive to the consequences of their actions, can learn that it is often not easy to decide what would be the right or just thing to do.

Children can recognize, also, that one can decide what would be the right thing to do in a particular situation and yet not have the will to do it. One question posed to a group of seventh-grade students in an ethics class in New York City was, "Pretend you are a doctor on your way to treat a group of children who have fallen ill with a serious illness in a neighboring town. You are notified en route that your own child has been stricken with the same illness. Should you turn back to take care of your own child or go on to treat the group?" Some youngsters said the doctor should go back to treat his own child; others said he should go on. But many of the latter group added that if they were in that spot they would go back to treat their child, even though they personally believed it was the wrong thing to do.

Opportunities for similar discussions frequently arise in the home, but parents often do not think to make use of them. We are apt to make a quick moral judgment rather than encourage our children to talk and reach their own conclusions. But children learn best, according to Professor Kohlberg, by working out their own responses. An eleven-year-old sees a thin, poorly dressed boy help himself to a pear from a fruit stand and comments half facetiously that if he were going to steal he would darn well take candy and not a piece of fruit! Then, reflecting on the child's appearance, he asks, "Do you think that kid stole because he was hungry?" This can lead naturally into a discussion: Is it ever right to steal? Do you think a hungry person might have another alternative?

Discussions like this are least useful when either parent or child is on the defensive; it is hard to learn when what we are really trying to do is prove we are right. On the other hand, if our child has done something we consider particularly kind or helpful, we can praise him and ask him for his reasons. For these talks to be meaningful, the child must be able to give his view without being criticized. Otherwise, he will go silent at the very first sign that we are "into that again." Let him finish. Parents should not show shock if his morality is somewhat primitive and should try not to end discussions with a moral or a point. The child should have a chance to weigh it all afterward. We can let him know how we feel without pressuring him into agreeing. He has to make his own way in his own good time to more sophisticated ethical thinking.

Learning from Mistakes

Our youngsters need to have the same chances we have had to make mistakes and learn from their mistakes. They need to be able to feel and think differently from the way we do, even when we are sure they are wrong! Frequently young people seem so contrary that parents conclude they have no influence at all. But even the most rebellious youngsters care what their parents think. They often become more willing to accept counsel when their parents become able to accept disagreement. And they will learn more from their mistakes if we can refrain from overemphasizing them.

Some parents have what their children consider extremely materialistic values. They are keenly interested in success, possessions, social position. What happens when such parents try to defend this way of life against a child's idealism, try to get him to become more "practical"? Generally, young people become disillusioned at this. As one older adolescent boy put it, "All my life they told me to do right—and now they tell me I have to forget everything they ever taught me if I want to 'get ahead.'" Parents who have sacrificed their own youthful idealism to make their way in the world may need to believe it was necessary. But maybe our children who have absorbed our hopes and our best ideals can find a better way to live. We ought to let them try.

People do not necessarily hate their parents just because they do not share their values. Actually, one often hears a grown man speak lovingly of his father's faults. But it is hard for our children to be relaxed about differences just now. We need to accept a certain amount of self-righteousness on their part.

Sometimes, however, children are seriously and justifiably alienated by their parents' different ways of looking at things. As put by one grown woman:

I finally realized that my mother would never value me as I longed for her to because she just doesn't value what I value. I'm proud of all the things I can do with my hands. I make my clothes, I refinish old furniture, and I have a green thumb. People are always bringing me forlorn plants they can't grow. But my mother just thinks of things like that as stuff you can get other people to do for you. It's my sister, a biochemist, whom she thinks of as her "smart" daughter.

Some parents have great respect for the son who earns a great deal of money or the daughter who marries a rich man but find it difficult to regard a child as successful where the rewards are not financial. Clearly these parents need to rethink their ideas about what is important. A child who feels "gypped" will not be strongly motivated to give others their due.

Working Toward Change

Our society seems to give less and less support these days to our best impulses. Corruption and selfishness are all around us. But many good people are trying to change things. And our children need to feel that

this is possible, that their lives can make a difference that they are not helpless. As Peter Marin and Allan Y. Cohen write, in *Understanding Drug Use: An Adult's Guide to Drugs and the Young*:

What the young need now are . . . parents . . . who side with their children against the powerful bureaucracies and myths that paralyze them . . . [who seek] not how to adjust them to things but how to find them viable alternatives.

We want our youngsters to feel that what they do matters, that *they* matter, that they can influence their environment. An attitude of "What's the use?" or "What can you expect?" or "You can't fight city hall" is discouraging. We need the energy and idealism of our young people to do battle with our immense social problems. When a young person hears on television or reads in the newspaper about a family displaced by fire or a recreation center that has been vandalized, he may feel the urge to help. And we ought to make time to encourage these efforts. Maybe he would like to look among his belongings for games or books or clothing to give. Perhaps he wants the chance to earn money to contribute. When a child can help like this, he feels that his efforts can make a difference. Parents often complain that children are self-centered, and they frequently are. But they can also be quite the opposite. It is a good idea to be alert to any expression on their part of the values we admire and encourage them.

Outside Influences

The family is not solely responsible for inculcating acceptable values in the young. Parents can expose children to a variety of situations in which values will be reinforced or extended. As Theodore Lidz writes, in *The Person: His Development Throughout the Life Cycle:*

> Society usually provides means of strengthening ethical standards as children approach and pass through puberty. The Scouts mobilize the idealistic strivings of youths and provide a code of ethics while seeking to interest the young adolescent in nature, as well as providing a favorable group set-

ting to offset antisocial gang formation.

Religious feelings become important and churches provide confirmation ceremonies with preparatory classes that reinforce ethical values. The adolescent with his new interest in ideals and idcologies can now find an interest in religion although it may have only bored him previously. He has need for such strengthening of his superego and he is beginning to seek reasons and meanings in life. . . . The youth now often experiences a closeness to God and feels that he has support and guidance in countering the temptations that are besetting him.

A basic moral principle—Do unto others as you would have others do unto you—assumes first that people must be aware of the consequences of their actions. The very young child who grabs a toy from a playmate is not yet able to realize that the other child will be unhappy as a result of what he has done. Later on, understanding this, he can become concerned about the consequences of his act. As a child becomes older, he becomes involved in more sophisticated situations in which the consequences of his actions arc not always apparent. Parents need to help children to see all the possible consequences of things they might like to do.

One of the most frightening aspects of modern life is that people can become widely separated from the consequences of some of their actions and may, therefore, contribute unknowingly to terrible events. Professor Charles Reich of Yale University speculates, in an article entitled "The Limits of Duty":

Let us follow the process of creating an evil more closely. A scientist who is doing his specialized duty to further research and knowledge develops the substance known as napalm. Another specialist makes policy in the field of our nation's foreign affairs. A third is concerned with maintaining the strength of our armed forces with the most modern weaponry. A fourth manufactures what the defense authorities require. A fifth drops napalm from an airplane when he is told to do so. The ultimate evil is the result of carefully segmented acts; the structure itself guarantees an evasion by everyone of responsibility for the full moral act. Indeed, the system, especially when it is combined with advanced technology, makes it unlikely that those who participate in the process will have any real awareness of the ultimate consequences. Neither the scientist nor the man in the State Department nor even the pilot actually sees the horrors of burning napalm on human flesh. The basic result of our system of doing things is to destroy awareness, alienate all of us from the consequences of our actions and prevent the formation of that very responsibility which has been at the center of our idea of criminal justice.

Parents often worry about the strong influence of their child's friends upon him at this age. Sometimes it seems as if anything a friend says has more weight than his parents' opinions. Prior to sixth or seventh grade, children look mainly to their parents for advice. But after that time the child's peers tend to have equal or greater influence on him. To some extent, this is an inevitable and healthy part of growing up. But parents may increase a child's vulnerability to pressure from his peers.

Many parents themselves overemphasize the importance of popularity, of being part of a group. Getting along with people, having people like you, paying attention to what other people think is often stressed by parents from the time the child starts school. Later, it is difficult for the same parents to pull back when their child insists something is all right because "everybody's doing it."

Spending Time with the Child

Then, also, parents in this country tend to spend less and less time with their children. In this way, many parents turn their children over to the children's friends. Professor Urie Bronfenbrenner of Cornell University makes the startling statement, in *Two Worlds of Childhood: U.S. and U.S.S.R.*, that children in the United States used to be brought up by their parents, but that this is no longer true.

While the family still has the primary moral and legal responsibility for the character development of children, it often lacks the power or opportunity to do the job, primarily because parents and children no longer spend enough time together in those situations in which such training is possible.

Something else is sought by our children to fill the void. In a recent study, 766 sixth-grade children reported spending during the weekend an average of two or three hours a day with their parents. Over the same period, they spent slightly more time than this with groups of friends and an additional two to three hours per day with a single friend. In short, reports Bronfenbrenner, they spent about twice as much time with friends, either singly or in groups, as with their parents. As Bronfenbrenner notes, "It doesn't take children very long to learn the lesson the adult world teaches, 'Don't bug us! Latch on to your peers!' "

Yet another, more disturbing result emerged from the same study. When the characteristics of the predominantly peer-oriented children were compared with those of predominantly adult-oriented children, the peer-oriented children reported engaging in more anti-social behavior, such as "doing something illegal," "playing hooky," lying, teasing other children. Clearly, says Bronfenbrenner,

> The vacuum left by the withdrawal of parents and adults from the lives of children is filled with an undesired—and possibly undesirable—substitute of an age-separated peer-group.

Bronfenbrenner, who refers to us as a "split society"—parents on one side, children on the other—regrets also the gradual disappearance of what is referred to as the "extended family": all the aunts and uncles and other relatives and friends who used to form part of a growing child's environment and his sphere of influence. These days many people settle in urban or suburban surroundings, often at great distances from

their parents and other relatives. A study made by Professor Herbert Wright and his colleagues at the University of Kansas showed that children growing up today in small towns still get to know a substantially greater number of adults in different walks of life than do other youngsters and are more likely to be participants in the adult settings into which they enter. The other adults in these children's lives "extend" the family, help reinforce values. Often, too, they fill in for a parent who cannot function well at a particular time.

Of course, the extended family can have its disadvantages. Novelist Ann Richardson Roiphe confessed in a recent article, "The Family Is Out of Fashion," that she

. . . would rather live in a swamp of stinging mosquitoes and biting crocodiles than spend a month with my very own blood ties. Because of educational differences, because of major value disagreements, because of the peculiar American experience that allows us to develop, peas from the same pod, into a multitude of fruits and vegetables so different from one another they can no longer cling to the same vine, we could no longer live together. We speak as many languages as destroyed the Tower of Babel. . . . It is no longer possible for us to reintegrate into an extended-family unit without violating the development of personality, of free choice, of education, of varied cultural growth that was so dearly won, so bitterly fought for by several generations of uneasy Americans.

There seems to be little doubt, however, that the greater the distance between parents and their children, the more the children will turn to their peers for sustenance and approval.

Friends Are Important

But even where parents and children have a close relationship, a child's friends are important. Some children are not members of a group or gang, either because they cannot find one that suits them or because they are not wanted or have other consuming interests. But for many young people at this age, the need to belong to a group is compelling, and they will make a great effort to achieve and retain a place in it. A young person gains from his group a feeling of strength and power.

People often think their child should be able to resist following the crowd. This is easier for a secure child, but how many are secure at eleven or even at fourteen? A child who has a feeling of his worth and place in the group can dare to be different. According to psychologists L. Joseph Stone and Joseph Church, writing in *Childhood and Adolescence: A Psychology of the Growing Person*:

It is not enough to say that young people should have sufficient moral character to reduce group pressures; failure to conform [even when the group is doing something one considers wrong] can produce feelings of guilt and inadequacy as severe as going against one's own conscience. Thus the group can place the adolescent in a double bind situation such that either of the courses open to him will lead to painful consequences.

Sometimes parents feel one particular child is a bad influence on their youngster, and this worries them. It is a good idea in a situation like this to give some thought to what our child is really getting from the other child. Sometimes parents misinterpret a relationship or misread a youngster. We may see our own child's good qualities, despite unattractive surface behavior, yet fail to see beneath another child's mask. Then, too, the child who looks "perfect" to us is not always so, as we ought to remember from our own youth. In some situations, a relatively stable child gives support to a "wild" one, and the relationship between them, with all its complexities, may contribute to the growth of each. When we criticize our child's friends, we are attacking his judgment. Accepting his friends tells him that we have faith in his judgment, and children tend to live up to our assumptions about them.

Dangers of Poor Choices

But suppose our child has a friend who steals, for example; what do we do? That depends. First, it is probable that all we know about this child's behavior comes from what our youngster has told us, which means that if, on the basis of information we get from him, we take action that he cannot tolerate, he may be less communicative in the future. Second, how does he feel about what his friend is doing? Perhaps he is disturbed that his friend's controls are that shaky and worries whether he will be able to control himself in this or other areas. Or perhaps he is sounding us out to see how we react. The best course is to state honestly how we feel about his friend's behavior, but not indicate that we feel the child is a candidate for Sing Sing. We have to judge what the friendship means to our child, discuss it with him, and let him decide how much to see of his friend. Antisocial behavior is not necessarily contagious. Psychologist Eda LeShan writes, in *Sex and Your Teenager: A Guide for Parents:*

There are times when it is a necessary part of growing up to live through a particular relationship. Much growth and learning about oneself can take place, even in some of the most ill-advised friendships.

The only real protection against poor friendship choices is whatever help we can give our children in respecting themselves so much that they are unlikely to choose relationships that will hurt or demean them, and that we help them to understand enough about human motivation and behavior to judge others with insight. . . . Surely if a youngster seems to be making one bad choice after another, we might conclude that his perception of his value as a human being is very poor, indeed, and under such circumstances we and our child need to seek help in taking a look at this pattern.

Although the influence of one friend can be strong, in general it is not as powerful as the pressure of a group, and it leaves the child more latitude to think for himself. If a child belongs to a group, many of whom are experimenting with drugs, for example, it is fairly certain that pressure will be exerted upon all to join in. Today, perhaps more than ever, parents are concerned about group pressures toward drug-taking, violence, and other dangerous behavior. We do not want our children to pay a penalty all their lives for making serious mistakes in adolescence. When a child's friends seem to be clearly destructive, parents will want to know what draws their child toward such a group, what he is getting out of it. Can we help him satisfy his needs in some other way? Are there opportunities at school or in the neighborhood for him to join other groups? Does he have a special interest or hobby that might be encouraged, which would involve him with other young people? We would want to be particularly welcoming to other friends at this point. If we decide we must put our foot down and insist that he stop seeing a particular group, we need to offer alternative possibilities.

When a child refuses to withdraw from a group whose members experiment with drugs or engage in other dangerous activities, the chances are that he is participating in these activities; parents need to face this. Professional counseling can often give helpful insights into such a situation and is worth considering.

Following the crowd is rather common at eleven or twelve, but as a child grows into adolescence it is good if he can learn to be somewhat discriminating, if he can begin to develop as a person who exists apart from, as well as in, a group, if he can begin to evaluate fads in fashion and ideas rather than accepting them whole. A youngster may continue to need the support of his gang for a while, but this need can coexist with a growing identity of his own. Parents help a child to resist the pull of the crowd when they support his struggle to think for himself, encourage his maturing judgment— even when they disagree with his views.

Who are the adults, after all, who do not need to run with the herd? They are mostly those who, over a considerable period of time, have developed faith in their own judgment and achieved the emotional strength needed to go their own way. To be able to stand apart from one's friends, one's neighbors, when one believes they are wrong requires great courage. This takes time to acquire. By sharing our lives with our child and supporting the best that is in him, we give him the best chance we can.

6

Changing
Attitudes
Toward School

CAUGHT IN THE pubertal undertow, many children
undergo profound changes in their attitude toward
school, their ability to work, their behavior in class, and
their relationships with their classmates. It is not surprising that a child's school hours reflect his physical,
emotional, and intellectual turmoil. What is going on
inside him, after all, does not cease as he walks through
the school door. It is probably more remarkable that
some youngsters perform as competently as ever during
those years, and that others come into their own, doing
better work than they have before.

But inner confusion, transient enthusiasms, moodiness, what educator Edward C. Martin refers to as
"general twitchiness"[1] take their toll of most children

---

[1] Edward C. Martin, "Reflections on the Early Adolescent in
School," *Daedalus* 100 no. 4 (Fall 1971): 1087–1103.

this age in one way or another. Suddenly a child will become uncharacteristically sloppy about his work, or sloppier than ever. He will experience a general slump in performance or in those courses he likes least. Or his work will show the same uneven quality, the same ups and downs as his behavior outside of school. Or a child who has always gotten along well with his teachers and tried to please them will become critical and rebellious: "Why does he make us do this?" or "What is the point to that?"

The parent's role throughout this period is difficult. Even understanding that a bad year at school is not uncommon for this-age child, we cannot just relax and wait for him to settle down again. We are afraid he will become accustomed to working at an inferior level, to poor study habits. We are concerned because marks earned during the last year of junior high school are considered for college entrance and may be important to his future. And we believe there must be something we can do to counteract his apathy or downright antipathy to school. We also perceive that some of his criticisms are right on the mark: this assignment does appear to be inane; that regulation does not seem to consider the students' feelings. But we may not know the school situation well enough to feel sure of ourselves here either.

Understanding the Problem

There are no easy answers to these school problems, and sometimes there are no answers at all. But in order for us to be of any help to our child we need to understand fairly well what is going on, both with him and at the school. Everything we have been discussing up to this point can shed light on the child's outlook. It is clear that the urgency of other needs can distract a child from concentrating on equations and intransitive verbs. This has always been true with youngsters of this age and does not exist because of the current state of American education.

Our child may feel that pleasing a teacher is for babies, that going along with adult authority is demeaning. Certain subjects may be seen as feminine or masculine and consequently a threat to a boy's or girl's efforts to establish sexual identity. Friends are an important part of school life, and problems in social relationships are also reflected in the child's attitude toward school. In many schools, the atmosphere is anti-intellectual; the popular and respected child is the one who excels in athletics or other extracurricular activities.

It is hard for the best schools to engage a youngster this age productively, and unfortunately, the average junior high school "by almost unanimous agreement, is the wasteland—one is tempted to say cesspool—of American education," according to Charles Silberman, director of a three-and-a-half-year study of American education commissioned by the Carnegie Corporation of New York, in his book *Crisis in the Classroom: The Remaking of American Education.*

Many junior high school children are faced every day with maddening rules, an inflexible administration, and teachers who are wasteful of students' time, who show lack of respect for them, do not trust them, do not allow them a measure of dignity, perhaps do not even like children. A great many junior high school teachers would rather be elsewhere, teaching high school, for example, and they leave when they can. The curriculum is frequently boring, and the sameness —every day every subject, very little variety—is deadening. Silberman says:

> Because adolescents are harder to "control" than younger children, secondary schools tend to be even more authoritarian and repressive than elementary schools; the values they transmit are the values of docility, passivity, conformity, and a lack of trust . . .

The child's individuality and humanity are repressed.

Sometimes parents tend to look at school complaints as did the father who said, "Look, I went to school, my father went to school, my son goes to school. Once in a while I loved it, lots of times I hated it. But I didn't think to run around complaining about it— or if I did, my parents weren't very sympathetic. My boy needs to do a little more work and a lot less lying around and all his school problems would be over."

Judging the School

It is hard for parents to know how to react to a child's grumbling about school, particularly when it really does look as if his problem is basically his own laziness or refusal to listen to his teachers. Silberman quotes a parent: "When my son was unhappy at Newton High school and doing poorly, I could never decide whether he was the problem or if perhaps he was right when he said that much of the school did not teach him anything." Now in an experimental annex of his old school, this boy has "an incentive which has focused his every bit of energy toward doing better today than yesterday and suddenly a hunger for many tomorrows which will enable him to do more."

This generation of American parents could decide not to tolerate bad schools, to sensitize themselves to what their children are experiencing.

A Visit Is Revealing

Of course, there are good schools and schools that are trying to improve, trying to find new ways to help children learn. Probably the best way to get a feeling for what is going on in our child's school is to go and see for ourself. Surprisingly, parents often resist visiting school, thinking, "What can I see in one morning?" or "They'll be on their best behavior when I'm there anyway." But we can learn a great deal in several hours. We can prepare first by listening to our child talk about school. If he has a particular problem, we can try to get a sense of what is at the heart of it so that we will know what to look for when we visit. If a child's complaints center around a certain area—specific regulations, school lunches, his history teacher—we can sit in on the class, join him at lunch, if possible. If this is not possible, why not?

We can take a walk around, observe the children changing classes. Do they seem at ease and cheerful? What is the relationship between the staff and the students? How do the teachers talk to the students? Are the halls and bathrooms clean? Are the books in the library in good condition? Do the students have a bulletin board for their own announcements? Must they get administrative approval for everything they post?

When we visit the principal, are the people working in the office welcoming? Does the school use parent volunteers as teacher aides, library helpers, tutors? Or are they wary of parents' presence? In classes, how do the children seem: alert and interested, or bored, listless, angry?

With what kind of feeling about the school do we come away? Is it too controlled or too chaotic? Does it seem that learning is taking place? How would we feel about spending six hours a day five days a week in this environment?

Do the teachers seem to see the students as individuals? The best teachers try to find ways to deal with students on a one-to-one basis. Are the children's complaints taken seriously enough by the teachers, by the administration? Are the children themselves taken seriously? One girl who complained about having to work in a group with a particular child was told jokingly that it would turn out all right because the girl she hated today would no doubt be cherished next week. This response made the child furious. She could have accepted being told that it was not practical to rearrange the work groups, but she was sensitive to being laughed at or treated as one of a species with certain defined characteristics—again not as an individual in her own right. A child does not have to find every subject pleasing, does not have to be happy all the time, indeed, will not be. But the impersonality of some schools, the feeling a child gets of being manipulated, pushed around, ordered about, herded, tears from his rights over himself, detracts from his possibilities as a learning, growing person.

Possibilities of Action

After a visit to school, we will know a great deal more about the kind of place where our child spends his days. Talking to other parents and children will broaden the picture further. We may find that our concerns can be divided roughly into two categories: the things we can try to deal with on an individual level with our child, his teacher, perhaps the guidance counselor or class adviser or even the principal; and those things of a broader nature that will require further study and concerted action by a parent group if progress is to be made.

Just how drawn into group activity we eventually become will depend on a number of factors: how bad the situation is, how active and effective the parents' association is, how much time we have to devote and what we feel we could contribute to their efforts, and so on. It is encouraging if other parents are willing and eager to work for change, much more difficult if they are apathetic and cynical about the possibility of making a dent, particularly in a large city school system. But parents' groups have been working with some success to bring about changes in many communities across the country. An organization can contact others for information and can raise money to send representatives to visit schools that are being run in new ways and achieving greater success in educating children.

But in the meantime, no matter what broad changes may be needed in the school, if our child is having trouble we need to deal with it now. Just how bad is it? Is he doing badly in everything, all across the board? Has he lost interest in school, just drags himself there, can't see the point of studying? Or is he having trouble only in one subject? Does he zip through his work, all haste and no head? Or does he spend long periods of time at his desk, staring out the window? How long has this been going on?

If he is achieving somewhere in his life, even at a hobby or music lessons or sports, this needs to be considered in the total picture. Can he concentrate on things he likes to do? What does he think about his work? Why does he feel he is not working up to par? What does *he* think needs to be done? How does he feel about his teachers? What impression does he give about his place among his classmates; does he belong, or is he pushed around or isolated? Children can be terrible to one another, and being "out" may cause serious school problems.

We will want to talk to our youngster's teacher or the school guidance counselor. This can be included in the earlier visit, or we may decide to take time to think about what we observed and discuss it with our child before talking with the appropriate people on the school staff. Either way, they need to be consulted. We can learn their impression of our child's behavior in school, how he gets along with his classmates, whether they feel he is working up to capacity, their estimate of his ability. How well does he read? Does he need special help in a subject? How does his work compare with that of the other youngsters in the grade? This conversation will help in evaluating the problem and may pro-

vide several valuable suggestions about helping our child.

A complete medical checkup (see Chapter 7), including hearing and eye examinations, will reveal if there is any medical basis for the trouble. The doctor should be told that the child has been having difficulty in school, so that he can be on the lookout for clues.

Educator Eric W. Johnson suggests, in *How to Live Through Junior High School*, that parents try to make an honest self-evaluation of their own role in their child's school performance:

> What are you doing that might be causing your child to underachieve? Are you too "managing"? Do you apply too much pressure? Do you provide emotional support? Do you respect him as a person? Do you condemn him too much? Are you too punitive? Do you set a good example? Do you provide intellectual stimulation?

Does our child believe in his eventual success; that is, does he feel that if he works hard he can do well in school? Professor Jerome Kagan of Harvard University, in *A Conception of Early Adolescence*, suggests that two thirds of the children in any class have "a barrier to serious involvement in the mission of the school" because of their rank. The top one third, he feels, expects success and is motivated by this expectation. The more competitive the school, the more the point is driven home. Junior high school is often a child's first experience with tracking, the grouping of people according to their ability. Says Professor Kagan:

This hard event forces each student to scrutinize his intellectual profile in some detail. Tracking often frightens those in the top track, many of whom do not believe they are talented enough to warrant the challenging assignment. It saddens and angers those in the lower track, who resent the invidious categorization and are forced to invent a rationalization against the importance of academic accomplishment. Once that rationalization crystallizes, it becomes incredibly resistant to change.

Do we feel our child lacks confidence in himself? How do we view his abilities? For some parents, doing well means that a child has to get 100 per cent or be the first or at least one of the best. Many bright young people don't *feel* intelligent because when they come home with an 85 on a test they are asked, "What did Johnny get?" or are prodded, "Next time, try for 90."

What kind of response does our child get when he shows us a written report? We do not want to encourage bad work or sloppiness, and if a youngster has obviously just slapped something together, we do him no service to oooh and ah over it. On the other hand, when he has worked hard with only partial success, we need to recognize and appreciate the effort. Most people, and children are no exception, are encouraged by warmhearted praise. And more often than not there are things to speak well of even when an overall effort is not up to par.

With a particularly sensitive child, we might have to go easy on the adverse criticism for him even to *hear* any of the good things we have to say.

142

Evaluation of the Child

Parents are sometimes so angry at children for not doing better that they allow themselves to confuse honesty with tactlessness, thoughtlessness. Naturally, a child needs to know our standards and values; what is in question is how strongly and how often. And standards cannot be absolute. They need to be standards for this particular child, and they need to be realistic and related to what he wants for himself. Every parent and every teacher knows that a barely passing mark may represent as much work and achievement for one child as an A for another. But most schools do not evaluate children on their individual achievement without regard to their standing in the class, or without competitive grades. The valiant effort of a C student to perform at the highest level of his competence is rarely valued as much as it should be. Does this mean that all C's should be valued as much as all A's? It depends on how well a child is using his potential. As a parent, our job is not to get an A out of a C student at any cost, because the cost is invariably too high. It is useful sometimes to ask oneself, "Will my comment be helpful?" Simple, but it is surprising what a stopper that can be for a lot of things one might otherwise say.

If a child disagrees with his placement for a particular subject, he ought to ask his teacher why he feels he belongs there. We may need to discuss this with the teacher as well. If we agree with our child, perhaps we could encourage the teacher to observe him specially for the next few weeks. Sometimes a child wishes to be with friends in another group, or does not want to make the effort to work hard in a subject, or dislikes the teacher of a particular section, or overestimates his ability. In these cases a parent, while being sympathetic, should encourage him to work where he is.

We do not want to denigrate extracurricular activities or successes. They are enjoyable and satisfying, which is important. We tend sometimes to think of our children as creatures in preparation for adulthood, rather than as persons whose lives now need to have meaning for them and be fun as well. In any case, working on a class play, playing on the hockey team, or helping to put out the newspaper require participation in a team effort and give important experience in working with others, in planning and executing a project from start to finish. Sometimes activities like these unleash a child's potential, show what he can do when he is involved in an area that he has chosen. And success in one field—in a school debate, chess match, baseball team, art competition, woodworking exhibit—encourages effort in other areas and builds self-esteem when his accomplishment is valued by people he respects.

When a Child Fails

Sometimes a child has simply not worked enough, and he fails. Failing under certain circumstances is more useful to a child than being pushed to study in order not to fail. He needs to be permitted to experience what happens when he does not work. If we pressure a child enough, we may get him through with a passing grade that he would not have achieved otherwise. But what about next year? What he learns now may keep him from failing in more important situations in the future.

Sometimes a child fails because he has bad luck. He has concentrated his efforts in an area the teacher barely touched on in the examination. It could have gone the other way had the test been arranged differently. We can point this out to the child. Suzanne Strait Fremon, in *Children and Their Parents Toward Maturity*, stresses the importance of helping a child understand all the factors that go into a situation—his ability, how much he has studied, luck, relationships among people. He needs to learn "how to take what happens and build on it." A child who is depressed about a failure—"What's the matter with me?"—can be helped to shift emphasis from himself to the matter at hand—What's the matter with his report or his understanding of algebra. Does he need to pay more attention in class, does he require special tutoring for a while? Can he use some advice about doing research or organizing his material? Mrs. Fremon suggests turning "I'm just not good enough" into "I'm not good enough yet" or "I'm not good enough *for that particular thing*." This kind of support strengthens a child.

Homework and Work Habits

Parents often complain that a child does not spend enough time on his homework. But time is probably used as a criterion too often. A child forced to spend an hour on an assignment often learns to "put in time" rather than to sit down, concentrate, and get the job done as well as possible in as short a time as possible. If he tends to let his homework go until he is too tired or has not enough time to do it thoroughly, he may need some structure imposed upon him. But the kind of regulation depends on why he has fallen into this habit. Are there just too many activities so that school work gets last call on his energies? Does he find it difficult to stop play and settle down to work? Then perhaps he ought to have a regular time each day for beginning his work.

Some people seem to have no hangups about work. If they have something to do, they are able to sit right down and do it. Others are not so fortunate. They put off work and concoct all kinds of excuses to do something else instead. Or when they do get to it, the slightest thing disturbs their concentration. Many of us vary in our work habits depending upon the job to be done. If we are efficient about the important things in our lives, the small things about which we procrastinate or are sloppy will not interfere too much with our functioning. A housewife who has no difficulty getting her daily chores done but always puts off writing letters is all right, but turn it the other way around and she is in trouble.

Our children will be working all of their lives, of which their early adolescence is only a part. We want to be careful that whatever we do now to encourage work does not do that job at too great a cost, does not compromise their capabilities thereafter. Without a lifetime zest for learning and working, all the information that can be crammed into a child during his school years will be useless by the time he is thirty.

The Problem of Distraction

Young people at this age, good students and indifferent ones, are frequently restless; when they try to concentrate, feelings, emotions, thoughts about other things crowd their minds, pushing out algebra and Spanish verbs. Sometimes parents insist that a child work in his room "away from distractions" when the worst distractions are inside him. A youngster often finds it lonely working off by himself. Can he study where we are ironing, or sewing, or reading? There is no reason why he should not write at the kitchen table while we prepare dinner, or in another part of the house where there is activity, if he is not bothered by it. Some people can get their work done amid all kinds of goings-on, and this should not be discouraged. To a person like this, what is onerous is banishment to peace and quiet, not the actual work he has to do.

If our child complains about the homework or has difficulty getting it done well on his own, it is possible the teacher's instructions are unclear. One hears the children on the phone many nights: "Did she want us to translate the sentences or just fill in the missing words?" "Were we supposed to read up to page 435 by this Tuesday or next?" Of course, often it is a matter of their not paying serious attention when the assignment is given. According to Eric Johnson, homework for the junior high school child should have four main purposes:

To give the student a chance to practice and master skills or content taught at school; to encourage or require independent creativity such as writing, doing projects or research; to encourage or require wide independent reading; and to provide time for reading "study" material in courses like history. . . . Homework should generally not be the learning of new concepts, new lessons, or new skills. These should be taught in school and homework used to reinforce them. Unfortunately, there are too many teachers who spend so much time "hearing" children "recite" on the previous night's homework that they haven't enough time left to teach the new material and consequently throw the responsibility for new learning on the child at home, where, if the child is puzzled, the buck is passed to the parent. If this is happening frequently in your school, a conference with the teacher or principal might be in order so that you may find out how you can help and incidentally, call attention to a condition of which the school may have been unaware.

Homework is not always valuable. A child may be right when he says an assignment is boring or useless. Our recognizing this and being sympathetic may be all he needs to help him through it, but if his time is commanded night after night like this, we will want to ask his teacher what she hopes he will learn from this work.

To Help or Not to Help
We all know well enough that we are not supposed to do our child's homework or write his reports for him, but many parents find it very hard to let their child hand in a less than perfect paper. So their contribution becomes more substantial than it should be. When this happens, a child may be pleased to hand in what he feels must be a better paper, but he cannot help but feel diminished by the situation. One boy reported that

his father had "the greatest ideas" and he knew his reports were getting better because of this—"I don't know what I'd do without him." We want to give a child a sense of his own strengths, not ours.

We can discuss concepts in math or physics or history in order to help him think through the problems more clearly. We can listen to his thoughts, ask him questions, read his work, suggest research sources. But the idea is to stimulate his thinking, not substitute our own. Many parents like to correct spelling and grammar errors, feeling that their child learns more if this is done at the moment when he is most involved with the writing. Teachers usually do not like this, believing they can help a child better if they are able to see what he can do on his own. But some are flexible enough to go along with a parent in this area and in others when the child is clearly learning and improving. One guide to how much assistance to offer might be to consider: Will my doing this make my child more or less likely to be able to do the next assignment on his own?

The Teacher

Our child cannot get the hang of the math this year; or he is suffocating under what seems like an interminable list of historical names and dates to memorize, and he has no interest in the period being studied; or he is suddenly unable to create an English composition, feels like a clod, and believes that the teacher so regards him. Is it his fault, or is it the result of poor teaching?

When a child has an inadequate or really bad teacher in a subject that is difficult for him in itself, it is a problem. He may be spending an inordinate amount of time working on or worrying about just this one course. Can the school offer any suggestions? Some schools will work with and advise parents who want to help their children with their work; others are completely hostile to the idea, sometimes with good reason. Parents frequently are able to stimulate their children's interest in certain subjects or to help them grasp new concepts or ideas, but much depends on the parent, the child, the relationship between them, the subject, and the school.

Are ideas and current issues discussed at home? Is our child drawn into talk about the connections between conditions in the past and the present? Between economic theory and how much a bar of chocolate costs? Is his opinion respected in family discussions? One parent said, "But Freddie says the most ridiculous things—if only he'd think it through before he speaks. How can we respect his opinions?" But a child will not join in family conversation if he is constantly made to feel stupid. If his ideas are listened to, he may be stimulated by a discussion to find out more about a subject. Sometimes children are shamed into studying, but in the long run this may detract from love of learning for its own sake.

Motivation to Learn

Motivation is a complex issue. One child told his social studies teacher that he could do better if he were more interested in the work. To which the teacher replied, "Perhaps if you put more effort into your work, your interest would increase."

Our children want to know why they are studying something, why it is necessary. Sometimes teachers skip this step, assuming, as in the case of grammar, for example, that the answer is obvious. Frequently young people are not respected enough to be told why a subject is important. Professor Kagan suggests that "the twelve-year-old is willing to believe that learning is valuable and that certain skills which seem irrelevant now are probably necessary for his role as adult." But he needs adults around him who believe in the importance of what they are offering him and can impart this belief to him.

Now that our children are studying material on a more adult level, we may find it interesting to read a few chapters of their history text or one of the novels they have been assigned, if we can spare the time. Young people are usually pleased at the idea that something they are studying is important enough to interest their parents, and this may heighten their own interest in it. Children generally work better if their parents value academic work. Even during these years, a percentage of youngsters continue to be well motivated to study. These are often young people who strongly identify with their parents' values and wish to please them. Parents who are concerned with intellectual achievements and who encourage academic competence help the school to compete with the distractions of this age.

Once in a while a child complains of a teacher who is cruel, who picks on him and makes his life miserable. We need to investigate, to talk to the teacher and, if necessary, the principal. Sometimes this helps ease things. But sometimes it doesn't, and the best thing we can do for our child, if we feel he is justified in his feelings, is to let him know that we are on his side. We understand. We can listen patiently to his complaints when he comes from school and sympathize with him. We do not like to undermine the authority of teachers, but children can understand the difference between a good teacher and a bad one, and we will not be lessening the effectiveness of his other teachers by upholding him when he is right. Mrs. Fremon believes that when parents lend support to their child in this way, it helps to "immunize" him against a cruel teacher's behavior; the teacher loses much of his or her ability to hurt the child. When a youngster knows that his parents are there and on his side, he experiences situations differently; he feels safer. As one boy put it, "Oh, they wouldn't do that to me—they know you'd be down on them right away."

Young people want a teacher to care about them "as a person," to be fair, and to have the ability to excite them about a subject and create an atmosphere in which they will learn. They want their teacher to know what he is talking about. Children often have an instinct for recognizing power that lacks authority and will puncture it when they can, while respecting true authority, indeed, seeking it out.

Going to school is our child's life for many years. Now, as he begins more and more to question the school's power over him and demand that it justify itself, we want to be listening.

7

Everyday Health Guide

E VERY PARENT KNOWS that for good health a child
needs plenty of nutritious food, exercise, fresh air,
sunshine, and sufficient rest. But living with a child on
a day-to-day basis reveals immediately that carrying out
this prescription is not that easy. A child growing into
adolescence presents special problems because parents
cannot control and supervise his behavior as much as
before—particularly as he reaches thirteen and fourteen
—and yet the youngsters themselves are not yet able to
take full responsibility for their own health care. Certain
things need to be insisted upon; others one may let
slide. But which is which?

Posture

For example parents—since the beginning of time,
probably—have been urging, "Stand up straight!" or
"Stop slouching!" To get some young people of this age
to stop slumping into chairs would require constant re-

minding, otherwise known as nagging. Is it worth it? What happens to them if they do continue to cruise around jaw forward, neck bent, shoulders hunched over? There is no evidence that this contributes to bad posture or curvature of the spine later in life. If a child's posture begins to cause him back pain *now*, that will probably motivate him toward improvement. Also, bad posture is not very attractive, and if we approach the issue from that angle we might achieve some results— more, perhaps, than if we talk about sitting up tall so that the internal organs have plenty of room, the blood can circulate freely, and the muscles can relax. All true, but it is hard to make this kind of information register with young people. Possibly the child does not realize how his slouched figure looks. He probably stands fairly tall when he checks himself out in the mirror in the morning. If he actually saw himself in a full-length mirror, slouched as he so often is, perhaps he would realize what he was doing to his appearance. On the other hand, this may be exactly the picture of cool sophistication he has been trying to achieve.

Girls who have grown taller faster than anybody else in the class traditionally hunch over until they develop some pride in their height or everyone else catches up with them. But the main thing with both sexes is that, since no functional damage is done, poor posture is not worth nagging about.

Acne

Many of us who were troubled by acne as adolescents used to think that if we ate a piece of chocolate it turned into a pimple. We might not have put it just that way, but if we succumbed to our terrible desire to purchase a chocolate almond bar (a double whammy: chocolate and nuts) on the way home from school, we started peering into the mirror the minute we got home to see if the pimple had popped out yet.

Now, scientists have conducted tests that indicate that neither chocolate nor other fatty foods, fried or otherwise, have any adverse effect upon the skin of adolescents. Of course, young people with acne, like other youngsters, require a well-balanced diet, but they need not forswear chocolate nut sundaes, peanut butter, or brownies until they are old enough to vote.

Acne cannot be blamed on dirt, either, or on masturbation or sexual fantasies, as was sometimes done in the past. It *is* caused by sex hormones, which are produced during adolescence at a suddenly increased rate. The hormones trigger the sebaceous glands to produce an oversupply of sebum or oil, which in turn plugs the ducts leading to the surface of the skin. Bacteria present on the skin enter the ducts and break down the sebum, producing fatty acids. If a person's skin is sensitive to this substance—usually an inherited tendency—acne occurs. It is not contagious. As the body achieves hormonal balance after the turmoil of adolescence, skin eruptions usually cease. Young people with acne should be told that it won't last forever.

Because acne is so commonplace and eventually stops by itself, parents often do not worry much about it. They may advise their children to "Try to forget it" or "Don't worry about it; that only makes it worse." Worry makes everything worse, acne included. Youngsters often break out at examination time, or just before an important party or a dance. But we cannot will ourselves to stop feeling upset. What we can do is take advantage of the many possibilities available today for prevention and cure of acne if a child is having a hard time because of it. Extreme cases may make a person feel so ugly that he hates to leave the house, and even one pimple can make a sensitive child miserable.

Care of the Skin

Whatever is important to general health is important to the skin also. Fatigue, anemia, infections all can cause flare-ups of acne. A well-balanced diet and sufficient rest are particularly important to a child with acne. Long before serious research was conducted into the causes and cure of acne, doctors noted that their patients' skin was always much improved after the summer. The rays of the sun or an ultraviolet lamp (in moderation) dry the skin, reducing oils and causing peeling, and also killing the surface bacteria.

Youngsters should be alerted not to pick at or squeeze pimples, as this increases the chance of scarring and may spread the acne.

If a youngster's scalp is oily, his hair ought to be washed several times a week and, if long, pulled back from the face, perhaps tied back at night, and his (or her) pillowcase changed frequently.

Daily skin care for a young person with acne should include washing *gently* morning and evening with warm water and a hypoallergenic soap. Hard scrubbing is irritating to the skin and tends to spread the infection. Steaming is helpful because it loosens pores. After washing, the child soaks a cloth in hot water, wrings it

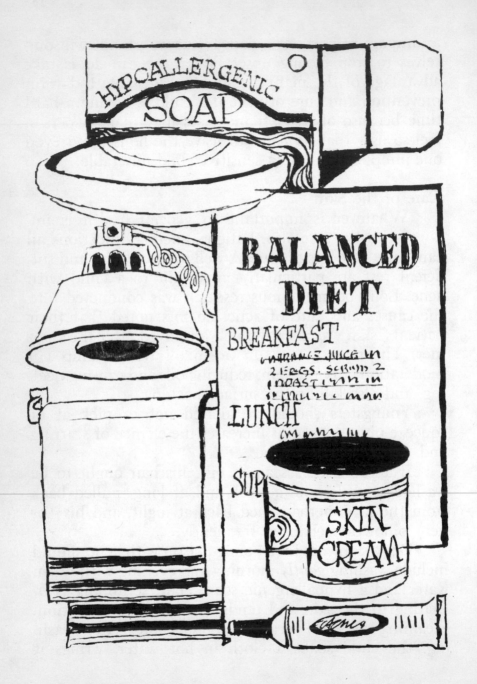

slightly, and places it over the pimples, repeating several times, then blotting with a clean towel. Facial saunas do the same job. After steaming, doctors recommend a mild astringent, applied with clean cotton, and then one of the medicated creams that help to dry the skin. These creams also do a good job of covering the pimples, camouflaging the redness.

If acne is severe and is not helped by these methods, a dermatologist should be consulted. He may try one of several antibiotics that have been found helpful. He can remove blackheads, and he can drain the pus from pimples to prevent infection from spreading. In extreme cases, there are other possibilities. If a child's face has become pitted or scarred, the dermatologist may recommend dermabrasion, or skin planing. One need not wait until the skin eruptions have stopped before having this procedure done. It is relatively minor and preferable to letting the scars accumulate until the end of adolescence.

Eating Habits

Somewhere around third grade for our children, many of us found that all our magazines began to disappear. Our children were appropriating them to cut out pictures of leafy green vegetables and brimming glasses of milk to paste in their nutrition scrapbooks for school. They were learning about proper diet, about nutrients, the importance of protein, the basic seven food groups. They started pressuring us to give them carrot sticks and celery stalks stuffed with cottage cheese, and they wanted to tape posters about good eating habits all over the kitchen walls.

What every parent of a teen-ager wants to know is: Where did all those carrot and celery-stalk lovers go? So much for brainwashing in the early years!

At eleven, a child is usually eating at least almost every breakfast and dinner at home, and we see what he is putting into his stomach. But at thirteen or fourteen and thereafter, a child may suddenly be rushing out without breakfast, be at a friend's for dinner, or even snack so much that he eats no dinner at all. There may come a point when a mother who has not wanted to be rigid about food and eating habits realizes that she has slipped from being casual to being lax—her child is really not getting enough of the proper foods.

During this period of rapid growth, a youngster's food needs are great. His protein and calcium requirements, for example, are almost double those of younger children and adults. He needs at least a quart of milk a day, in one form or another, and plenty of food rich in high-quality protein, such as meat, poultry, fish, cheese, and eggs. Those large appetites are normal and need to be appropriately satisfied.

The average child who does not eat enough of the right foods, however, still may continue to gain in height and weight. Thus, if his parents explain to him the dangers of poor nutrition, he is likely to retort that he doesn't feel his bones melting or his hair falling out just yet. We stress that he is increasing his susceptibility to infection, and he comes back that he has not had a cold in months. We explain that food is energy, fuel to run the body, that if he does not get enough of the right fuel, he may lack energy, feel tired, get headaches. And he acts as if he cannot comprehend the connection. It is truly a rare child of this age who will be impressed by a discussion of nutrition.

Getting Through to the Child

The situation now is not hopeless, though. For one thing, knowledge about nutrition is one of those things children sometimes absorb without being willing to admit it. If they are put in possession of the facts they may decide to eat somewhat differently, but they're darned if they will respond to that "Drink another glass of milk, Freddie" baby stuff. If a child feels low in energy he may—when he understands the relationship between pep and what he eats—start paying more attention to what goes into his stomach. If he knows that insufficient protein or calories may stunt his growth, he may be moved to improve his eating habits. If her hair is not as shiny as she would like, she may think twice about the connection between lustrous hair and what she eats.

Our job, then, is to let our children know what foods they should be eating, and why, without getting their backs up. Perhaps pictures of leafy green vegetables and the rest of the basic seven on the kitchen wall? We tend to nag our youngsters to eat certain foods or not eat other foods, but we rarely think of giving them a short refresher course on nutrition at a receptive moment—or at several appropriate moments over a period of time.

Why does he need to drink milk if he "eats all that ice cream"? A significant percentage of teen-agers suffer from calcium deficiencies. Ice cream and other foods derived from or made with milk are good for a child.

But in order to obtain the calcium in one quart of milk he would have to eat two quarts of ice cream, or six cups of cottage cheese, eight servings of pudding, four ounces of cheddar cheese, or about twelve servings of cream soup. These foods are excellent, but it is clear that a youngster needs to drink milk (unless he is allergic to it) if he is to fulfill his daily calcium requirement without resort to medically prescribed calcium pills. If a child dislikes plain milk, keep trying until you find a flavor—chocolate, coffee, strawberry—that will make it palatable to him. Would he drink malteds, hot cocoa, milk shakes?

Our children do not have to worry about cholesterol because their bodies do not store it at this age. That is fortunate, because eggs, in particular, are an all-round food rich in various nutrients.

A daily vitamin pill, while it gives leeway, does not make up for a really inadequate diet. Food has certain values that are not in vitamin pills.

The Importance of Breakfast

Studies of students and workingmen have shown that those who eat no breakfast or a nutritionally poor one tire more rapidly—late-morning slump—and do not think, study, learn, or work as well as they could if they had eaten properly. A good breakfast should include fruit or fruit juice, egg, buttered toast, milk, and cereal, too, if the child is hungry for it.

If a youngster frequently dashes off in the morning —"Sorry, no time for breakfast, gotta run"—perhaps we could help him organize himself so that he has more time.

If a child says he just is not hungry that early in the morning, he should be encouraged gradually to acquire the habit of having a good breakfast. Perhaps he could begin by taking only a piece of fruit or a glass of juice for several days, then add cereal or buttered toast and so on. After a few weeks, he could be eating a full breakfast —if he wants to.

Lunches and Snacks

Lunches are important, too. A midday meal that is low in protein but high in sugar and starches tends to produce quick energy, but when the sugar level of the blood drops later in the afternoon, the child feels tired, perhaps headachy, pepless. If a child takes his lunch from home, we can pack it with an eye to the nutrients he needs. We can add cheese to the luncheon meat in his sandwich, give him nut-raisin cookies instead of vanilla wafers, stick in an apple or a pear or a banana, remember that a chocolate bar with fruit and nuts has more protein and vitamins than a plain one, and so on.

A child need not have every nutrient he needs at every meal, but over the course of several days his diet should work out to be balanced. Ideas other mothers have used to interest their adolescents in nutritious snacks are the following:

• Keep soup in a pot ready to heat when everyone comes home famished from school. Soup and crackers or buttered toast are filling and nutritious, and particularly popular in the winter.

• Put snacks in individual, attractive, covered refrigerator dishes for eating right from the container, and vary them: one day individual custards, one day cut-up raw vegetables (not just the usual, but string beans, peas and pea pods, cauliflower, cherry tomatoes, accompanied by a paper cup of creamy salad dressing to be used as a dip). Don't forget color; serve green, red, orange, white, add a sprig of parsley, dill, watercress. The more attractive nourishing food is, the better it can compete with the empty-calorie foods that youngsters find so tempting.

• Have plenty of fruit and vegetable juices prepared and waiting in colorful pitchers. Never overlook the importance of convenience. Even having to add water to a can of frozen concentrated juice may seem like too much effort to a child after a day at school.

• Keep a supply of mixes and dips—liver pâté, minced sardines sprinkled with lemon, deviled eggs mixed with olives or pickles or pimiento—to be eaten with bread, crackers, or chips; whipped cream cheese for date-and-nut bread, and so on.

Of course, pies, butter cakes, butter cookies, and the like contain nutrients, too, and children love them. They are all right when eaten in moderation and when they don't spoil the appetite for meals. Needless to say, they are high in calories, which is fine for some children, less so for others.

Of the snacks that young people buy on the run outside the home, popcorn, potato chips, and peanuts are better for them than most cookies and candy. And, of course, fruit juices from the vending machines are a better idea than carbonated drinks.

When asked about candy and soda, many physicians advise parents to forbid the use of both, since they have little or no food value, are bad for the teeth, and spoil the appetite for the nutritious foods a child needs for health. But it is extremely difficult to banish candy and soda completely from the diets of young people. Some parents are able to motivate their children to substitute foods containing natural sugars such as those found in fresh fruits, or the synthetic sweeteners found in low-calorie soda or sugarless gum. These are preferable to candy and other products sweetened with sugar containing sucrose, which are harmful to the teeth. When children themselves become interested in preserving their teeth or reducing their weight, they are more apt to want to eliminate such empty calories from their diet.

Overweight

A great many young people between eleven and fourteen are overweight. Sometimes it is just "puppy fat"; a child puts on a little extra weight around ten or eleven and then, often without any particular effort, loses it or "grows into it" by the time he is fifteen or sixteen. Other children become too heavy at about this age because they indulge in too many high-calorie foods and too little physical activity.

Still others become overweight before puberty and probably will be after it, unless they do something about it. They can lose weight, but the problem has to be approached in a special way. One startling fact has emerged from the most recent studies of this group of adolescents: the great majority of them eat less than the average child of their sex of normal weight. Yes, less!

This is so revolutionary an idea that most people simply do not believe it. Why, then, are these young people overweight? Because they do not move about nearly as much as thin people. Even when playing a sport such as tennis or volleyball, they move slowly and are often standing still. Why this should be so is complicated and not yet fully understood. But it seems clear that their bodies do not utilize fats and carbohydrates as they should. Too much fat is stored and too little energy is provided for the child, which is why he does not feel like being more active. Unfortunately, this lack of physical exertion results in even less fat being burned, and the cycle perpetuates itself.

Exercise Is the Key

The crucial factor, according to Dr. Jean Mayer of Harvard University, who has done pioneering research in the treatment of overweight, is exercise. Since most of this group of overweight adolescents have become that way because they are abnormally inactive, it is vital to get them moving.

Every overweight adolescent would do well to consider how exercise can help him. A 15- to 20-minute walk, for example, burns up about 100 calories, roughly the amount contained in two cups of popcorn.

Most people think of weight only in terms of what we eat, but weight can be lost by increasing the expenditure of energy as well as decreasing the intake of food. There is a belief that exercise is worthless in control of overweight because, it is thought, the more you exercise, the hungrier you get, the more you eat—and there you are, back where you started. But this is not necessarily true. And it is not true for the many overweight adolescents whose activity level is significantly lower than it should be.

It is difficult for any adolescent to find time for a lot of exercise each day, and the overweight teen-ager may find it harder than others to walk, run, do indoor exercises, engage in sports. He needs to push himself, but it will begin to come easier after a while. For those who are willing to undertake an hour of exercise a day, the rewards can be great. An hour of bicycling or fast tennis will cause a weight loss of one pound a week—a good rate of loss—without any change in eating habits. The same is true of an hour and a half of Ping-Pong or three quarters of an hour of swimming (but not just floating or sitting at the edge of the pool!). Dr. Mayer suggests a daily walk of about an hour and a half at the brisk pace of four miles per hour for that one-pound weight loss.

Jogging, bowling, baseball, skating also help—the type of exercise does not matter. What is important is that it be regular. If one or both parents are overweight, and since the tendency to overweight seems to be inherited, this is likely to be true, they can engage in these activities along with their child, especially on weekends. Exercise is good for us all. It makes the body more firm, improves muscle tone, and helps posture, as well as increasing one's feeling of well-being. A great deal of planned exercise may seem laughably impractical for your family, but one important fact should be considered. Exercise is a positive approach to losing weight, difficult, perhaps, but not necessarily unpleasant. Dieting is negative, involving deprivation. Whatever can be done to eliminate or ease the amount of dieting is probably worth trying.

Dieting Safely

Until an overweight child becomes active enough to burn up what he eats, he will need to cut down on foods that are high in calories but low in protein, minerals, and vitamins. These include sugar, candy, soda, cakes, pies, and other rich desserts. A child who is overweight needs a balanced diet and the same nutrients as an average child. But he cannot have as much leeway with high-calorie extras. When a child's doctor has ascertained a need for weight loss, he can recommend a safe caloric minimum and a good daily diet, taking into account the child's rate of growth and development and his energy expenditure.

Crash or fad diets can be harmful. Misguided attempts at reducing are a major cause of anemia in adolescents, and they seldom work in the long run, anyway. All studies show that unless everyday habits are changed, weight lost is gained right back.

Weight loss should not be rushed. A pound a week is a sensible goal. The child needs energy to get through his day. If he diets too strenuously, he will be tired and move even less, which is what we are working against. We need to remember, too, that his bones are growing, his muscles are developing, his teeth are forming just like those of the normal-weight youngster. Serious damage can result if he goes for too long without getting enough of the important nutrients.

A child should never be given diet pills without a doctor's prescription. It is preferable, of course, to help him lose weight without getting him on a routine of pills.

The parent of an overweight child has an even

greater need to learn about nutrition. And we need to debunk dietary myths. Toasted bread *is* just as fattening as plain bread; thinly sliced bread is less fattening only because there is less of it; water does not make a person fat; margarine has the same caloric value as natural butter. We need to learn to plan meals and snacks for the most pleasure and the least calories.

Planning the Diet

Library shelves are filled with books and pamphlets offering ideas on meal planning and recipes to make dieting more interesting and less painful. The Bibliography suggests a few that are particularly pertinent for young dieters.

Emphasis always should be on changing eating habits, substituting lower-calorie foods for higher caloric ones, not simply depriving a child of all sugars and starches. A dieter needs interesting, varied, fully satisfying meals just as everyone else does, perhaps more.

The following are some suggestions to help a child lose weight:

• Having dinner ready at a regular time each night may make a child less likely to snack. On the other hand, it sometimes works out well to give a child five small meals instead of three larger ones each day to reduce hunger and the feeling of deprivation—or three meals and two regular, planned snacks, one after school and one before bedtime.

• Skipping meals is a bad idea. It causes fatigue, and generally a person eats twice as much later on to make up for it.

• Learn how to make tempting low-calorie desserts and

snacks. Keep a container filled with low-calorie, ready-to-eat snacks in the refrigerator. For ice cream sodas use low-calorie soda, skimmed milk, and dietetic ice cream and fruit flavorings.

• If the child's doctor has put him on a diet of a certain number of calories each day, and he loves to snack, he could reserve a certain amount of his daily calorie allowance for snacks. Then, if he is going to be in a situation, such as a party, in which he expects to be tempted, he could utilize an idea suggested by *Seventeen* magazine—the "snack bank"—saving some of the calories allowed for snacks for several days or even a week in order to splurge on a special occasion.

• Do not use food as a reward, an expression of affection, or a solace for troubles. Substitute noncaloric treats instead: trips together, activities and sports together, gifts that are not related to food gain or loss. When you are tempted to bring home a cake, bring home a treat from the five and dime instead.

• Give praise when weight is lost but loving support all along that does not depend on weight loss.

• Let the child know that other children have successfully overcome weight problems.

• Explain that there will be times when, although he is continuing his regime faithfully, no weight is lost. If these plateaus are expected, they will be less discouraging.

• Encourage new activities that involve his moving around—taking up a new sport, walking to pick up his kid sister at school, doing some of your marketing, mowing the lawn, vacuuming, or whatever active job you can think of for him to do on a regular paid basis.

Perhaps having a dog that has to be walked would help.
• Boredom increases the temptation to overeat, so it
helps to encourage substitute occupations for hands that
yearn to pick up a piece of candy. Would the child
like to begin organizing a stamp collection, learn to
type, build a model, learn to knit, do needlework, hook
a rug, paint, model in clay?
• Chart his progress, providing short-term goals. Perhaps the child could set up his own goals, aiming
toward a certain loss per month or by the time vacation
begins. Other kinds of incentive may also help him to
lose weight: saving money he would have spent on
sweets to buy something he wants, working toward a
specific goal in a sport or in exercises at home.
• Has he an overweight friend who would like to go
on a diet and might exercise with him? The buddy system is probably one of the most effective aids to losing
weight.

It is helpful when weight reduction can be super-
vised outside the home, through a reducing club at the
Y or at school, a weekly weigh-in at the doctor's, a summer camp program for overweight youngsters. In this
way the parent's role can be just that of appreciator of
progress, encourager, ardent supporter.

If a parent is overweight, too, he should remember
that making fun of himself for being fat demeans the
child as well. If the parent feels hopeless about losing
weight, this makes the child feel pessimistic about his
situation.

Parents of overweight children often act in many
ways, usually without realizing it, to sabotage the dieting effort. The child should not be urged to take sec-

onds, to taste a freshly baked cake, or to break his diet "just this once."

The best impetus to reducing is a child's motivation. If he does not really want to diet and exercise, his chances for long-term success are not good. We should not be angry with him for eating or for not exercising, or ridicule or humiliate him for being clumsy or fat or because his clothes do not fit. We should not berate him for sitting around too much or nag him to exercise or be more active or more social. Making an overweight child feel worthless or depressed is not difficult, but it is not a successful dieting technique. And we do not want to give him the impression that our love depends on how big or small he is.

Getting Enough Sleep

A child who cannot drag himself out of bed in the morning is not necessarily a youngster who has not had enough sleep. Some people are never peppy when they first get up, no matter what time they went to bed the night before. It is later on during the day that a parent can judge whether a child is getting enough rest. Young people this age generally require about nine or ten hours of sleep a night. But their needs vary. If a child is getting less sleep yet does not seem tired, perhaps he is able to manage with less rest than most people. It is an enviable ability.

Few children like to go to bed, and adolescents are no exception. Often a child wants to get more rest, plans to get to bed earlier, but cannot seem to settle down. He jumps up to make another phone call, raids the refrigerator for another apple or the cupboard for a cookie. Then he remembers some homework that he decides he should do. Or he settles down early enough but he has so much on his mind that he cannot fall asleep. He "can't stop thinking." He is "trying" to fall asleep but can't. He may worry because everyone else is going to bed and he does not like to be the only one in the house awake.

Limits about bedtime, as discussed in Chapter 4, are important. But when a child has trouble getting enough rest because he is tense or overstimulated, it is little help if all we can think of to do is get tough about his bedtime. Perhaps we can both try to figure out how he can arrange his life to get the rest he needs. We have to start the conversation on the right note, because otherwise he will claim that he is *not* tired, he *is* getting enough sleep, and the conversation is all downhill after that.

Identifying the Problem

Sometimes the problem is complicated by a child's poor sense of time, of how much he can accomplish in any given fifteen minutes or hour. He leaves something to work on between 8:30 and 9 that will take him at least an hour and a half to do. He is probably a person who can never correctly gauge how long it will take him to do an errand or come home from a friend's house. Perhaps we can interest him in doing a time study for a week, keeping a record of important tasks he performs, writing down time started and time stopped. He may learn something that will help him.

If he regularly procrastinates about doing a particular task—his math homework, a certain chore—we want to learn why.

A youngster may be worried about school, friends, home life, himself. These problems become interwoven, too, as when tension makes him feel tired so that he does not sit down to his homework as early as he should and then is not ready for bed until late and is tired again in the morning. Helping a child with his problems, as discussed in Chapter 8, may help him to get more rest as well.

Parents and child share a common interest: the child's health and well-being. In families sometimes this mutuality of concern is forgotten; parents fight with their child to do things "for your own good," and the child angrily tells his parents he is doing something such as drinking milk "for *your* sake, not mine." A young person has to begin to take responsibility for his own health, for doing what is good for him for his own sake. And we need to work *with* him to accomplish this, not, as it sometimes seems, *against* him. In any case, we ought not to let our concern provoke us into nagging him about sleep or about other health matters. Sooner or later, this is self-defeating.

Fatigue or lack of energy may have other causes besides insufficient sleep. Poor diet, rapid growth, lack of exercise, illness, or emotional problems can all make a youngster feel listless. A physician should be consulted if the situation does not improve in a reasonable time.

Sometimes it is helpful if a child can get into the habit of going to bed fifteen minutes or half an hour early and then listening to music or the ball game on the radio, or reading for a while. A regular nightly routine is in itself soothing—laying out clothes and school

things for the next day, perhaps having some warm milk or cocoa and crackers.

Cigarettes

Many young people do not seem to be deterred from cigarette smoking by the known risks of cancer and heart disease. While the percentage of adult smokers has been decreasing, the percentage of teen-age smokers has been increasing, and the percentage of twelve-year-old boy smokers has doubled in recent years. Many young people smoke because they are trying to look older; others are responding to pressure from their group; still others find that the aura of danger attracts rather than repels them. Smoking is part of the devil-may-care ambiance they are trying to cultivate. Even if they think seriously about the risks, they mistakenly believe that they can always stop before they are old enough to get into trouble with their smoking.

Recently, however, there has been evidence of lung damage to teen-agers who smoked cigarettes for only a few years. Breathing tests given several hundred Connecticut boys and girls who were regular smokers revealed abnormal lung function. Although some of this damage may be reversible if the youngsters stop smoking, it is possible that there are effects, such as arrest of lung development, that are permanent. Obviously, smoking reduces endurance and breathing capacity and is a risk young people should be encouraged to avoid. The American Heart Association reports that teen-agers are much more likely to smoke if their parents do.

Seeing the Doctor

As our child grows older, he may resist going to his physician for a regular checkup. He feels fine, he says, so why bother? But a friendly, trusting relationship with his doctor cannot be sustained if they see each other only in moments of crisis. At some point he may have a problem he feels he cannot discuss with his parents, or that only a doctor can answer. Then it may make all the difference if he has a doctor with whom he feels comfortable. His physician also will want to keep an eye on how he is doing, to catch problems that need treating, to offer guidance concerning habits that may affect his health now or later on in life.

What Should a Medical Checkup Include?

The doctor will take a comprehensive history of the child and his family. If he is seeing the child for the first time, he will ask a long list of questions about him from birth onward. He will want to know, for example, about past illnesses, operations, accidents. He will ask if there is a history in the family of a specific disease such as diabetes. If a physician has seen the child before, he naturally need only be brought up-to-date.

The doctor will then inquire about the child's general health, his habits, and his way of life. How much sleep does he get? Does he sleep well? Does he have plenty of energy, or does he tire easily? A child this age should be peppy; if he is not, the physician will want to find out why. Does he have a good appetite? Is his elimination regular? Does he take any medication? Has he had allergic reactions to medication in the past? Other allergies? Does he have frequent colds? Sore throats? Headaches? How does he get along at home? At school? Has he been depressed lately? As the doctor talks to the child, he is also studying him.

The physician also gets clues to possible hearing or visual defects. He notices posture, skin, general appearance. He asks about complaints, symptoms, problems.

The physician will also order laboratory tests. In a complete urinalysis, the urine is tested for albumen (to detect abnormalities of the kidney such as nephritis) and sugar (a screening test for diabetes). It is examined under the microscope for abnormal cells that might indicate kidney or urinary-tract infection. Among blood tests, a hemoglobin or hemacrit test is given to screen for anemia. The Tine test screens for tuberculosis. There is a significant increase in active tuberculosis during the prepubertal growth spurt.

When a physician has done a comprehensive history, physical examination, and the above tests, he will detect most of the things that can be detected about a patient in this age range. Other special tests may be ordered if there is some specific indication that they are needed.

Immunization

If a child has already been immunized against polio and measles, the American Academy of Pediatrics makes no further recommendation with regard to those diseases for this period. Many doctors, however, do give a polio booster every four years. If a child has neither had measles nor been previously immunized, he should receive the vaccine now. In addition, a child may need to receive once during these years a combination booster for diphtheria and tetanus. Because diphtheria is not the menace it once was, some parents have become lax about immunization. Serious outbreaks have occurred in recent years, however, because the germ that causes diphtheria has not been eliminated from the United States. The D-T booster should be given ten years after the child received his last one. The American Academy of Pediatrics presently advises revaccination against smallpox every six years, but physicians expect this recommendation to be revised soon because smallpox is so well controlled. Many pediatricians do not routinely give it this often. Because mumps can be very painful if contracted during adolescence and can cause sterility in males, many pediatricians recommend that children who have not yet had the disease be given the mumps vaccine. There is controversy as to whether adolescents should be immunized against rubella (German measles). In earlier childhood, both boys and girls should be immunized, chiefly as a public-health measure to help eradicate the disease from the community. Many physicians feel that teen-age girls who have not previously had the vaccine should be immunized, whether or not they have had a supposed case of the actual disease in childhood. Others do not immunize because of the danger of giving the vaccine to a girl who is pregnant, and because it is not yet known how long the immunity conferred by the vaccine will last. If it wears off after three, five, eight, or even ten years, young women will be unprotected as they leave their teens. Accordingly, it may be recommended in the future that a booster be given at the time of marriage. Immunizing adolescent boys is not so essential, although most authorities feel that they, too, should have the vaccine.

Other immunizations are required only if a child is going into an area where a particular disease is endemic.

The Final Conference

An important part of the checkup, during which the pediatrician discusses his findings with parent and child and makes his recommendations, is the final conference. At this stage of a child's life, a checkup may produce anxiety. The child is more modest, for one thing, and also may be so concerned about his development that he takes a doctor's grimace as an indication that something is dreadfully wrong. A doctor who understands young people will make a point during the conference of saying, "Everything is in order, all according to schedule," or something by way of reassurance. If a young person seems concerned about any aspect of his development, the physician will reassure him, explain what is necessary, and give him an idea of what to expect in his development in the near future. Sometimes the doctor may be able to anticipate difficulties and will then discuss preventive care.

As a child begins to be more mature, a physician usually likes to see him alone for at least part of the checkup. Then, with the reassurance that his questions have no punitive intent, he can ask in a straightforward way about school, drugs, sex, or other matters.

Doctors are particularly concerned today with drug use. Many will begin by asking about cigarette smoking and then go on to inquire about a child's possible use of medicines in general, such as antihistamines, aspirin, tranquilizers. Then, if the child looks drawn, sallow, has lost weight, is jittery, or too talkative or too quiet, he will probably ask directly about other drugs.

If a physician has a good rapport with his young patients, they are likely to ask him direct questions concerning their sexual problems or fears. Or, if a doctor feels that a child is anxious about some aspect of sex, he will draw him out, discussing masturbation, petting, intercourse, the possibility of venereal disease, pregnancy, or whatever he feels is indicated.

A good doctor will encourage a child to talk about himself. Symptoms that the youngster might otherwise be embarrassed or reluctant to mention may be important.

The American Academy of Pediatrics suggests a checkup every year, or at least every two years. Of course, a physician may ask to see a child more often if an aspect of his health requires more frequent supervision.

Years ago, many pediatricians used to stop seeing children when they reached their teens. Today it is becoming more common for the pediatrician to follow youngsters through adolescence, and many now have special hours for seeing adolescents so that the teenagers need not sit in the waiting room with babies and younger children. Sometimes a child himself asks to change doctors somewhere along the line for one reason or another. A youngster ought to be able to talk easily with his doctor. He should have a doctor of the same sex if that is important to him. When a child does not wish to be cared for by a pediatrician any longer, he usually goes on to an internist or a general practitioner. A girl often consults a gynecologist as well. In recent years, a new possibility has been added: the specialist in adolescent medicine, a physician primarily concerned with the problems of this age group. Many large cities now have adolescent clinics, where pediatricians, surgeons, internists, gynecologists, psychiatrists, psychologists, social workers, and nurses work as a team to provide health care and counseling for young people.

8

Adolescent Misery

D O PARENTS CAUSE adolescent misery? No. But many parents tend to make it worse. And many parents help ease it. What distinguishes between the two?

Not love. Most of us love our children and want them to be happy. We do not like to see them moping around or irritable or downright miserable. We do not *plan* to embarrass or infuriate them or constantly get their backs up.

A saintly disposition is not the answer, either. All parents have their clashes with adolescent children. This time of life, says anthropologist Ruth Benedict in *Patterns of Culture,* is as "definitely characterized by domestic explosions and rebellion as typhoid is marked by fevers."

Nevertheless, there *is* a quality that sets apart the relationship of some parents with their adolescent children—good communication. That quality in the life of the family eases pain, softens hurt, and helps a young person to be more optimistic about his future.

Recently *The New York Times*[1] printed a little exercise for adolescents. The questions went like this:

Do your parents wait until you are through talking before "having their say"?

Do your parents seem to respect your opinion?

Do your parents tend to lecture and preach too much?

Do you discuss personal problems with either of your parents?

Do your parents talk to you as if you were much younger?

Do they show an interest in your interests?

Do your parents trust you?

Do you find it hard to say what you feel at home?

Do your parents have confidence in your abilities?

Do you hesitate to disagree with either of them?

Do you fail to ask your parents for things because you feel they'll deny your requests?

Do they really try to see your side of things?

Do your parents consider your opinion in making decisions that concern you?

Do they try to make you feel better when you're down in the dumps?

Do your parents explain their reason for not letting you do something?

Do you ask them their reasons for the decisions they make concerning you?

---

[1] Millard J. Bienvenue, Sr., "Why They Can't Talk to Us," *New York Times Magazine*, 14 September 1969, p. 86.

Do you help your parents to understand you by
telling them how you think and feel?

Obviously, the exercise is designed to gauge the relationship between young people and their parents. If
a child feels that his parents lecture him, do not really
try to see his side of things, and do not try to make
him feel better when he is down, he has little incentive
to discuss his problems with them. On the other hand,
a child who believes his parents respect his opinion,
trust him, and make it possible for him to disagree with
them is more likely to let his parents know what he is
thinking and feeling and to talk to them about the
things that really matter to him.

What is at the heart of a good relationship is, of
course, good communication, and in this sense the questions are particularly revealing. Many a parent says,
"How I wish my son would tell me what's bothering
him," or "I would so like my daughter to confide in
me," or "I'm sure I could help him if he would give me
the chance." Such parents need to look at what happens when their child does talk to them.

Suppose a thirteen-year-old comes home from
school really downhearted after losing a class election
for student-council representative. He lets his parents
know how hurt he feels, although he probably put up a
cool front at school. How do his parents react? Consider the following possibilities:

• They use the opportunity to give him some advice that
they think will be helpful to him in the future. If he
has any hope of succeeding in school politics he had
better soften his critical attitude toward his schoolmates,

an attitude much in evidence at home in his behavior toward his younger sister and brother. They help him to analyze his failure and to see what he is doing wrong so that he will have better luck next time.

• They try to cheer him up by playing down the defeat, saying that the student council does little anyway, and in any case he has to learn not to take things so hard.

• They try to cheer him up by assuring him that it was all for the best since he needs the time to study, having done badly in math this year.

• They say: "You're lucky it wasn't worse. You'll do better next time. You'll get over it; this time next year you won't even remember it. You shouldn't feel so bad. You *can't* really feel so bad. You shouldn't worry."

• They rub in the fact that they have been telling him all year he would never be popular if he kept refusing invitations to parties and other social gatherings.

The poverty of the last possibility is blatantly obvious. Although many parents cannot resist "rubbing it in," most of us do realize that this is not a helpful approach. But the other responses are also lacking. None are altogether helpful; some would be extremely irritating.

What They Want from Us

A parent who tries to make light of a defeat, political or social, or to convince a youngster that it was all for the best, may feel that he is being sympathetic and understanding. But when a person is hurting he needs a soothing balm—not advice, not criticism, not analysis, and surely not reminders of other failures. He should not be made to feel guilty or unmanly for feeling hurt or pressed to feel better right away. We need to deal with his immediate feelings first. Then, later, the child can look ahead, accept reason. It is important not to gloss over a hurt, writes psychologist Dorothy W. Baruch, in *How to Live with Your Teen-ager,* or to try to pretty it up or turn it, presto, into cheer. And telling a person not to feel what he does never makes the feeling go away.

An approach that recognizes his feelings—"What a shame! You must be disappointed. I know you had your heart set on it"—shows the child we understand. It tells him, also, that it is all right to have the feelings he has. Such an approach helps him to recover.

As a child grows into adolescence, he often becomes more secretive, less confiding. There are things he just does not wish to discuss with his parents. But a child whose relationship with his mother and father is nourishing to his spirit, to his self-esteem, will tend to remain in good communication with them, to let them know when he needs them. If, no matter how sympathetic parents feel, the child does not come home with his problems, they should consider how they respond to him.

The Need to Be Appreciated

Our son shows us a story written for school. It is imaginative, even funny, but all those spelling errors are like red flags in front of our eyes. He is fourteen, for heaven's sake! "Can't you use the dictionary when you're not sure how to spell a word?" we explode. So this bright youngster does not feel like the author of an imaginative and funny story. He thinks of himself as a dud who will never learn to spell.

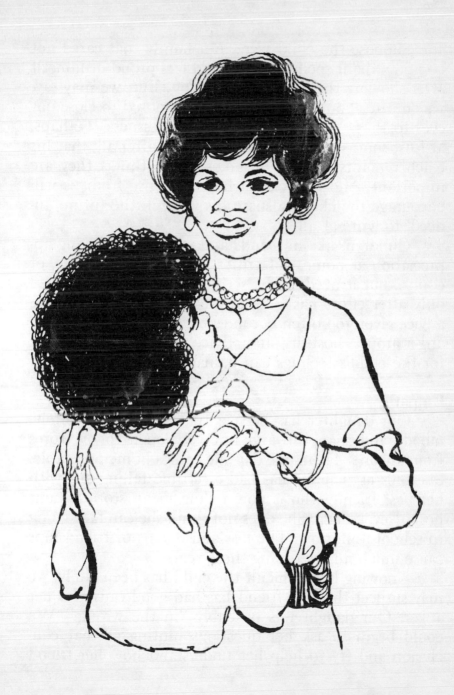

Suppose the child were in a family that cared not two pins about spelling. He would feel proud of himself after showing them this composition. But, we may say, we *do* care about spelling. Are we supposed to close our eyes to those glaring errors, that carelessness? Perhaps, at least some of the time. We assume, after all, that his teacher points out his mistakes if she thinks they are important. And it is clear which response from us will encourage the child to share his work in the future, indeed, to write at all.

Children, like husbands and wives, need loving appreciation at home, not critics. Advice has its place, of course, but it needs to be sensitively timed and offered only after effort has been appreciated. What is more, advice given too often becomes nagging, advice given in anger arouses hostility, and advice given without respect for the child's feelings can damage self-esteem.

Empathy

Our daughter has been a trial to live with lately, moody and snappish, and not very open to overtures from anyone. Then, one day she comes home miserable. She tells us that she has had a terrible falling out with her best friend, who is now telling mean stories about her to "everyone." She does not think she can face going to school tomorrow. The ups and downs of friendships cause much misery during these years.

Knowing how difficult the child has been lately, we may suspect that the friend has had good cause for her anger. Our daughter is probably "in the wrong." We could begin to ask her questions hinting at that conclusion and try to help her understand how her friend must have felt. Or we could reassure her that there are other girls, that everyone will forget all about it in a day or two. And, after all (as the tears continue to flow), it is not the end of the world. "For heaven's sake, if you get yourself into such a state over something like this, how will you ever handle big disappointments?"

All of these words are familiar to parents, who have themselves been children and been exasperated to hear them from *their* parents. They may be "right," they may be sensible, they may be said with reasonably good intentions, but they don't help much. A child comes to know he will be offered this "routine" and tends to keep even more to himself.

Do we hear how we sound when we go on this way? We ought sometimes to listen to our own words, our own tone of voice. It is a way of putting ourself in our child's shoes and learning how it feels.

Their Suffering Is Real

Perhaps one of the reasons that we lose touch with our children at this age is that we do not really believe they are as unhappy as they frequently seem. How could they be? Most of us, if we think someone is making a fuss over nothing or next to nothing, cannot work up much sympathy. It is a rare person who can feel for someone even though he himself sees the other's troubles as slight, or self-inflicted, or even humorous.

We see our children as having their whole lives ahead of them, with crucial choices as yet unmade, destinies as yet undecided. They are looking forward to romantic love, instead of backward at it, as their parents may be. It is difficult for parents not to feel a little envy of their children, particularly if some of their own choices have turned out badly, if their own destinies are less than satisfying, their own sex lives on the wane.

It is hard not to be impatient if we feel they exaggerate their difficulties and dramatize minor aches. One hindrance to communicating well with our child may be an understandable lack of empathy with the troubles of this time of life. It is hard to be supportive when deep down we feel they've got it good! Can we try to feel with them and accept the truth: that their pains are real, their suffering is genuine?

Universal Miseries

Such feelings are shared by adolescents the world over. How they are manifested and directed depends on the culture in which the child is growing up.

Psychologist Norman Kiell writes, in *The Universal Experience of Adolescence* that if we could reach back to the emotions of our own adolescence, we might be more understanding, but most of us cannot. The pain of adolescence is such that most people forget how it was with them then. Says educator John A. Rice, in *I Came Out of the Eighteenth Century:*

. . . but where is one who does not wince at the memory of his adolescence? . . . Women say they cannot remember the pangs of childbirth. Crafty nature blots them out, lest there be no more. So also one does not remember one's second birth . . . from childhood into youth. This second birth . . . becomes in memory a dull pain.

Perhaps everyone else is maturing, but he is not—no signs of growth. Or no one else is maturing yet, but her breasts have become an embarrassing protuberance under her sweaters. No use to tell her that in one year she will be pleased about her body. Right now she is *different*. She is certain people are *staring* at her. And we talk of a year from now; why, we might as well be speaking of an eon!

This does not mean we should not let a child know that it won't always be this way. Tactfully done, it may help a little. Sometimes it helps, too, to arrange an opportunity for an early-maturing daughter to spend some time with a somewhat older cousin who has been through it all recently, or an adult with whom she has rapport.

Reading May Help

Books about young people undergoing similar trials can be reassuring that one is not alone. *The Diary of a Young Girl* by Anne Frank, although written while the thirteen-year-old Dutch girl was in hiding from the Nazis during World War II, offers striking insights into the turmoil of the adolescent spirit. Constantly in conflict with her mother, although her father was "a darling," she wrote one night:

> I'm boiling with rage, and yet I mustn't show it. I'd like to stamp my feet, scream, give Mummy a good shaking, cry, and I don't know what else, because of the horrible words, mocking looks, and accusations which are leveled at me repeatedly every day, and find their mark, like shafts from a tightly strung

bow, and which are just as hard to draw from my body.

I would like to shout to Margot, Van Daan, Dussel—and Daddy too—"Leave me in peace, let me sleep one night without my pillow being wet with tears, my eyes burning and my head throbbing. Let me get away from it all, preferably away from the world!" But I can't do that, they mustn't know my despair, . . . I couldn't bear their sympathy and their kindhearted jokes, it would only make me want to scream all the more. If I talk, everyone thinks I'm showing off; when I'm silent they think I'm ridiculous; rude if I answer, sly if I get a good idea, lazy if I'm tired, selfish if I eat a mouthful more than I should, stupid, cowardly, crafty, etc. etc. The whole day long I hear nothing else but that I am an insufferable baby, and although I laugh about it and pretend not to take any notice, I *do* mind. I would like to ask God to give me a different nature, so that I didn't put everyone's back up. But that can't be done. I've got the nature that has been given to me and I'm sure it can't be bad. I do my very best to please everybody, far more than they'd ever guess. . . . [I'd like to] try for *once* to be just as disdainful to them as they are to me. Oh, if only I could!

When parents believe in the pains of their children, this creates a rapport between them that eases the intense loneliness the young person feels. Of course, an adolescent rarely believes his parents can truly understand him; obviously they have never felt what he feels.

But he is encouraged by their support and warmed by their concern, although he may not always show it.

Handling Moodiness

Parents do not have to, should not, cannot tolerate all moods, all outbursts. A child needs to be aware that there are limits to what is tolerated in the household. And there must be room, too, for a parent's moods, feelings, and concerns. But we want to offer as much of a haven as we can.

A girl bursts in the door after school. Her mother says, "Boy, you seem full of pep this afternoon."

And she responds, "Do you *have* to talk like that all the time?"

"Like what, for heaven's sake?"

"You just make me sick, that's all."

At which point the mother, if she is in A-one condition, will be alert enough to realize that she has done absolutely nothing to deserve this outburst. Her child has had a hard day at school and obviously needed to explode the minute she reached the safety of the nest. If the mother's sagacity and cool persist, she will not react defensively with the "What did I do?" approach, knowing full well that this will only impel her daughter to think of some way to justify her outburst and that the dredged-up complaint may drum up a full-scale battle. She will not comment on the child's irritability, either, because this, too, will make matters worse. The girl will deny indignantly that she is grumpy, it is her mother who is impossible, and so on.

What the mother does say and do naturally depends upon the child, what has helped in the past, and what the mother herself feels capable of at the moment, having perhaps had a rather hard day herself. Sometimes it works just to ignore the words, mention that there is a milkshake freshly made for her in the refrigerator, and retire from the combat zone for a discreet period.

To let a child go too far is not good for either of us. She will feel guilty, and we will begin to feel like a sacrificial lamb. It is a good idea to act before we are so angry that we find ourself counterattacking, to stop the child firmly while we still remain fairly calm. If we cannot, if we are pretty hot-tempered ourself, then she will have to face our temper, and that is not so terrible. Sometimes parents who remain icy calm throughout any scene drive their child wild; the child may continue to provoke in an effort to force an expression of feeling. But our anger should not be so uncontrolled as a child's. That is, we should not attack a youngster's personality, looks, or ability. We confine ourself, if possible, to the child's behavior at present, which should, in any case, leave us plenty of ground!

"Instant Tradition"

Typical of this age is "You never . . ." or "You always . . ." Any parent can fill in the blanks. It is called instant tradition. The child cancels out all the ways we have tried to be helpful and understanding in a blanket condemnation not only of our present behavior but also our past actions and past concern for him. (Parents also are sometimes guilty of this, and, needless to say, it is not helpful when we do it either.) It really does little good at a time like this to take him literally. He does not actually think that we never do anything to please him or always make scrambled eggs in the morning when we know he prefers boiled. Such gross exaggerations had best be accepted with equanimity. Of course, the trouble is that an accusation often has a small grain of truth in it. Many of us tend to respond guiltily. "Do I really make scrambled eggs more often than boiled?" we ask, appalled at ourself. However, the issue probably is not scrambled eggs versus boiled, so we need not waste too much time on it. Maybe our son is upset about something totally different; he needs to let off steam at someone, and mothers are, alas, very convenient. Or perhaps he is feeling deprived in relation to his sister (the scrambled-egg lover) or by life in general; he picks on eggs when he has something else in mind.

We need to absorb a certain amount of rudeness and irritability during these years, stopping short of martyrdom, of course, without doing battle.

Probably the most difficult problem for most parents to cope with is unpleasant behavior whose particular target is us. As our children grow into adolescence we, mirrored in their eyes, lose all our charm, our taste in clothes, our tact, our conversational élan, anything we ever thought we knew. For parents who are not secure in their feelings about themselves—and how many of us are?—this is especially painful. We cannot tolerate it with the sense of humor and sunny disposition that we may display toward his other foibles.

His criticisms hurt; they pierce our most vulnerable parts. We feel disliked, even hated. We also feel like failures. We have been told that this is the way all adolescents are, but when *our* child rejects *us* it is intensely personal.

Why They Reject Us

Why does it happen? And can it be avoided or softened? Along with the upsurge of sexual feelings accompanying puberty, explains psychiatrist Theodore Lidz, in *The Person: His Development Throughout the Life Cycle*:

> . . . there is some reawakening of . . . the sensuous and affectional attachments to the parent of the opposite sex. . . . The boy may now begin to idealize his mother and find nothing wrong in commenting on how beautiful she is and seek ways to please her and gain her affection. . . . Then, as the real upsurge of sexual feelings gets under way, the youth begins to turn away from his or her attachment to the parent, unconsciously and sometimes consciously concerned by the sexual aspects of the attraction. He begins to find fault with the parent, criticizing him or her, convincing himself that the parent is not attractive and not an object worth seeking. The criticism also spreads to the parent of the same sex.
>
> The girl is apt to dream of being a woman more capable than her mother, a person more attractive to her father, and may begin to talk to her mother in rather condescending tones, sorry for this "has-been" who has passed her prime.

So it happens that our children sometimes reject the very people they most need and love. For even while they are constantly finding fault with us, they love us, too. And there are moments when they feel guilty because of their feelings about us and miserable because they know they have hurt us.

Accepting Their Attitudes

A parent who likes herself as a woman (or himself as a man) and has a sturdy inner core will manage better during the upheaval. And he or she can offer more support to the child, whose safe passage through adolescence is immeasurably aided by the emotional availability of his parents. It is helpful to the girl and her development, for example, says Dr. Lidz:

> . . . if the mother is not angered by the condescension and can allow her daughter to indulge in . . . fantasies of being a more desirable female and potential sexual partner than her mother. It helps the girl gain self-esteem and enables her to feel capable of relating successfully to boys.

If the father can accept the fact that his son will be better than he is in some fields and not regard his boy's development as a challenge to his position, the boy can be encouraged to develop his strengths without fear.

Our children do envy their parents' position as the decision-makers, holders of the purse strings, heads of the household. And a lot of their rebellion reflects their feelings of helplessness in the face of this power. Then, too, while we are feeling that we can never strike the right note with our child, he may feel the same about us. When he wants to talk, perhaps we are rushed or in a bad mood. When he is busy doing his own work, we want him to stop and help us. When he wants to act grown up, we treat him like a baby. When he acts baby-ish, we tell him to act his age.

Fostering Better Communication

Sometimes a direct approach is helpful: "We really have been growling at each other lately. Is there something at home that's getting you down?" Or, simply, "Is something the matter?" or, "Is there some way I can help you?" If a youngster does respond, we should be receptive and patient, try to appreciate how things look from his viewpoint. Perhaps there are changes we can make to ease things for him. Young people who will not come clean about what is troubling them, assuming that they can put a finger on it, often complain that it never helps to try to talk to their parents. Nobody ever listens. It just starts a fight; nothing ever changes. A child who is willing to talk it over has not given up. He still believes his parents care about him and hopes to get along better at home.

Adolescents frequently feel that their parents do not like them very much. More often than is realized, a wide gap exists between the way parents feel about a child and the way the child perceives their feelings. "How can he possibly feel unloved?" a parent will ask. But the parent, though truly loving, may on a day-to-day basis criticize, nag, find fault, grump, and rarely express love affectionately.

We should try to make openings for easy talking and be flexible enough sometimes to drop what we are doing when a child wants to be with us alone, without his brothers or sisters around. We can make a habit of

dropping into his room to chat at night before he goes
to bed, or of taking long walks, or going biking on weekends. Possibilities depend on the family's interests and
working schedules. Perhaps we can watch baseball or
football on television with him; maybe he can show us
how to develop photographs, and when the work is
finished we can relax together over a snack in the
kitchen. Perhaps we can learn a sport or a game together, or a craft, at home or at a class given locally?
Working with him on his stamp collection or another
hobby, playing checkers or chess or other games, painting a room or making curtains or knitting scarves for

every member of the family are other possibilities for joint activity. Every mother and father can come up with ideas especially suited to themselves and their child. Working or playing together, we and our child get a chance to talk without "making a big deal out of it." We are, in effect, creating unhurried, unpressured, agreeable situations where communication between us is likely to flourish. Some of these ideas take a lot of time, others a little. We do what we can, but most of us can find a half hour every day or an hour several times a week to simply enjoy being with our child.

Other Helpful Approaches

It also works wonders for a child's morale to be pampered and catered to occasionally, especially when life is particularly rough. Gestures of warmth make a difference, an unexpected offer to help him with something he wants to do, for example. We need not wait for a special occasion to give him a present. Candy he loves, a gadget from the five and dime, something attractive to wear, stationery printed with his name, a record of his favorite rock group, a magazine concerned with his special interest, two tickets to a ball game or a concert—all convey warmth, concern, love. A word of warning: We should not give clothes or objects that reflect a taste or interest we wish the child had, but which he has resisted!

Often a relative or friend of the family with whom the young person has a rapport is able to be helpful, and we should encourage such contacts even though it is hard not to be a little envious when our child can unburden himself to someone else, but not to us.

Serious Problems

If people at any other time of life behaved the way these youngsters do, they would be considered abnormal. The extreme shifts in mood, the periods of intense depression followed by elation, the outbursts for no apparent reason, the unreasonableness, are "normal" only in the context of this period.

But not all behavior can be shrugged off as "adolescence." Some behavior, although not uncommon at this point, is nevertheless cause for concern. Dr. Fritz Redl writes, in *Pre-adolescents—What Makes Them Tick?*":

> After all, there are such things as juvenile delinquents and psychoneurotics, and we shouldn't pretend that everything is bound to come out in the wash.

The idea of a child's "growing out of" difficulties is sound enough when the problems are simply "growing pains." But when serious problems persist over a considerable period of time, we cannot take them lightly. Says Dr. Redl, if a child's disturbing behavior

> is too vehement and impulsive, too unapproachable by even the most reasonable techniques, then the chances are that Johnny's antics are symptoms not only of growth but also of something being wrong somewhere and needing repair . . . definitely serious, hangovers from old, never really solved problems, results of wrong handling, wrong environmental situations or other causes.

Some signs of serious trouble are frequent running away from home, chronic truancy, behavior that is too withdrawn or too aggressive, compulsive overeating accompanied by overweight, serious learning difficulties. One should also be concerned about disturbing traits that persist for a long time or seem to go very deep. For example, intermittent cruelty to a brother or sister is not uncommon or abnormal, particularly now when intense, troublesome feuds do tend to develop. But continued, frequent acts of cruelty or acts that actually threaten the safety or emotional well-being of the younger child cannot be shrugged off.

We may become so accustomed to quarrels or lack of civility that we regard a child's behavior as ordinary and are perhaps not alert to the fact that his depression has gone on too long unrelieved, or his demands have become more and more unreasonable, or his bickering has developed a malicious undertone. Very often a child signals that he needs special help by blatant antisocial behavior such as shoplifting; but a youngster who cannot make friends over a period of time or "just can't concentrate" on his schoolwork may need help just as much.

We are closely involved with our children, and sometimes for that reason alone may fail to evaluate the situation clearly. Dr. Redl advises:

Whenever you are very much in doubt, it is wise to consult expert help for the checkup—just as you would in order to decide whether a heart murmur is due to too fast growth or to an organic disturbance.

9

Money:
Earning It
And Having It

EVERY NEIGHBORHOOD HAS some children who are re
sourceful enough, and want money enough, to
create jobs and businesses for themselves.

Steve's *personalized* newspaper delivery service.
Your papers delivered every day on time—never
torn or wet. Try me!

What did you forget at the store today? I will go
to the store for you. 50¢ for ten items or less. See
Joe Gibbs, apt. 7B afternoons after 3:30

Homemade bread fresh from the oven, orange bow-
knots, chocolate fudge cake and other good things
to eat. Susie's catering service. Only the best of in-
gredients are used and no mixes. Ask for my price
list. Orders require 24 hours notice. Weekends only.

Unfortunately, many people do not have confidence in youngsters this age. The average eleven- to fourteen-year-old (not without some reason!) is considered less than responsible, less than serious, and less than capable by most of the adult population.

When asked if she would subscribe to Steve's personalized newspaper service, for example, one woman answered, "I'd like to help Steve out, but you know kids. Next week he'll decide it's too hard to get up that early in the morning and I'll have to go back to my old delivery service."

Susie had similar trouble with her catering service. It was difficult at first for people to believe that a thirteen-year-old girl could bake cakes, breads, and cookies that were as good as one could buy at the store. Since Susie had learned to bake from a superb cook, namely her mother, she *was* good, and word-of-mouth soon provided her with many customers. She had underpriced her goods, however, and she had to go out of business after a few months of spending half of her weekends slaving for too little reward.

Eleven-year-old Joe was never able to drum up enough business for himself. Surely there must have been many people in his large-city apartment building who needed last-minute items from the store. But they never called on Joe, perhaps because they had visions of his losing their money, crushing their loaves of bread, or breaking their eggs.

Steve's newspaper business did thrive eventually, earning the fourteen-year-old money for a camera, a tape recorder, a trip to another city, and enough after-school snacks to sink anybody but an adolescent boy.

Their Reasons for Working

Why do children work? That's easy, they would say. We want more money. What do children gain from their work? More than money. The family wage earner is usually endowed with added respect and authority. Success is often measured in terms of earning ability. Being able to earn is a recognized badge of maturity. The youngster who begins to earn money, especially on a regular basis outside the home, has reached a symbolic point on his journey to adulthood. And while children work for the cash, the effect on their self-esteem is, in the end, the more meaningful fruit of their labor.

If we can do a needed job and do it well, every one of us derives satisfaction. When the job has a monetary value to someone else, the satisfaction is enhanced, and all the more so for young people, for whom it is a new experience. They begin to feel more important; they refer to "my job" in front of others. Youngsters who hold a job often have a special cachet among their peers. They are thought of as more grown up.

Youngsters rarely feel that their parents give them enough money. However adequate their allowance may be, being able to add to their income through their own efforts gives them the feeling that they can help themselves, that not everything in their lives depends upon being in their parents' good graces. As we have seen, this is of crucial importance to children who are growing into adolescence.

A boy has an absolutely desperate need for a new racing bike, but his parents feel that his old bicycle should last him through the end of high school. The situation is not hopeless, however. He can work to get his own racer. A girl wants a polo shirt with a cupid design such as all her friends wear. But her mother says, "No, there's not enough drawer space for all the shirts you have already." Nevertheless, she can work to earn it.

The discipline of doing a regular job, on a regular basis, on his own, helps a young person to see himself as a responsible, capable, and reliable person. Although parents want to be available for advice if needed, the more a child can manage on his own, the more satisfaction he will derive from the experience.

When Steve began his newspaper delivery service, his parents could not believe that he would get himself up at 6:15 every morning. But they resolved, nevertheless, not to interfere. They felt that if he lost customers because he could not drag himself out of bed to make deliveries on time, that in itself would be a learning experience. On the other hand, if he had to rely on his parents to push him out the door each morning, he would be robbed of an essential source of satisfaction— doing it on his own.

Values Beyond Money

As it happened, Steve surprised them. The business had been his idea, and he was determined to make it succeed. Although he already had a wind-up alarm clock, he took money from his savings to purchase an electric alarm and set the clocks to ring five minutes apart each morning. He got himself up, he got himself out, and he got the papers to his customers on time every day. Carrying out his own project in his own way, by himself, made him justifiably proud of himself and enhanced his feeling of self worth. His parents found him more willing to try other new things, unconnected with work, as a result of his increased self-confidence.

What if a child cannot manage on his own like this? Sometimes it is because the job was his parents' idea, not his, or because he did not have a realistic picture of what the job involved or of what he could manage. Helping a young person evaluate a project *is* a parent's job. We need to discuss with him what is involved and listen to his ideas about how it can be done. We should not push a child into something or hold him back because of lack of confidence in him. At the beginning, a child would probably be better off taking on a simple, small job that he obviously can handle, rather than attempting a complicated arrangement where success is questionable. On the other hand, if the child himself has conceived the larger project and his parents have made sure he understands all that is involved, they will probably want to support him. There is such a thing as going into too many "what ifs" and "you'll nevers!"

Because a youngster's job often involves manual labor, such as mowing lawns, washing cars, or assisting with carpentry, he is likely to develop a respect for people who work with their hands, to see that "blue-collar" jobs can be difficult and tiring and can be done well or badly, just like other work. These are no small fringe benefits.

Granted the desirability of paid work, what kinds of jobs can young people of this age get and do? Work around the house is usually the easiest to find, although parents and children tend to disagree about which jobs should be paid for and which should be considered "chores" or work that the child contributes to the household. A chore, suggests Eric W. Johnson,

. . . is something a child hasn't the right to refuse to do (like making his bed) and which you would not have to hire someone else to do. On the other hand, a *job* is something he would have the right to refuse (like painting a room) and which you would hire someone else to do. By this definition, chores should not be paid for, and jobs should.

Naturally, in a family where both parents work and money is tight, children of this age, particularly of thirteen and fourteen, will be expected to pitch in with baby-sitting, preparations for dinner, and other household chores that would not be considered part of the child's regular responsibilities in another family.

Jobs that many children do for money in their own homes include baby-sitting, shoveling snow, mowing grass, raking leaves and other yard work, gardening, cleaning the garage, washing and polishing the car, ironing, mending, preparing school lunches for all, preparing dinner one or more times a week, preparing breakfast, taking a younger brother or sister to a weekly music lesson, listening to him practice, cleaning the cellar, cleaning kitchen cabinets, washing the insides of windows, and other odd jobs.

Many of these jobs are also performed for neighbors. In answer to a questionnaire circulated by Eric

Johnson, junior high school students listed the following among their paid jobs: deliveries, wood-chopping, taking inventory in stores, caddying, washing windows, painting, repair work, vegetable picking, delivering prescriptions for a drugstore, tutoring, and taking care of plants or pets while their owners are away. They also mentioned businesses that they had developed either alone or with friends, such as growing and selling plants, selling old paper, selling greeting cards, carpentry, and professional photography.

Should Working Teen-agers Contribute?

If they are earning their own money, should young people have to contribute to the expenses of the home or be given a smaller allowance? If the family needs the child's help, then, of course, he should be expected to contribute a portion of his earnings. This would be particularly true of thirteen- and fourteen-year-olds who have a greater earning capacity. It does not seem right for a child to have a substantial earned income that he can use for entertainment and still receive an allowance if his parents have a difficult time just paying for family necessities.

But most parents in comfortable circumstances do not expect children of this age to contribute money toward family expenses. The big job of these young people is school, and their contribution to the household is usually in the form of regular chores performed without pay—bedmaking, dishwashing, and the like. If they choose to find paid work, they generally are not required to take a reduction in their allowance. When a child cannot enjoy relatively free use of money he earns at this age, his incentive to work is dulled. On the other hand, the few who earn fairly large sums may want to contribute to an unusual expenditure, such as a special vacation, but this should be their own decision. Children ought to be able to work for what they want, just as their parents can.

Should the money a child earns or receives as his allowance be entirely his own, to squander or to save as he sees fit?

To answer this question we need to ask why a parent would want to regulate a child's spending or have him account for what he does with all his money. The responses are generally that a child cannot be left to learn to manage money on his own, that the child who is profligate with what he has does not necessarily learn to spend sensibly through continually practicing the opposite, that parents need to keep track of what their children are doing with their money, that children ought to make charitable contributions, learn to save, be directed toward wise purchases, and so on.

Learning to Handle Money

How do people acquire their ways with money? How did we? From imitating (or rebelling against) a parent? From parental guidance through our childhood and adolescence, or trial and error as adults, or perhaps both? The way some adults deal with their financial affairs makes one question their qualifications for imparting wisdom on the subject! Can a mother who is wildly extravagant teach her child to budget? Maybe. But sticking to a budget requires not only knowledge but also a certain temperament. We may see in the same family a boy who saves carefully, plans each expenditure, and a boy who buys on impulse the most impractical gadgets or treats all the guys to sodas. But their ways of managing money would not be the only differences between those two brothers. A child's way of handling money reflects his personality just as everything else does.

A parent complains, "That kid can't hold onto money; when he's got it, it burns a hole in his pocket until he blows it all on something worthless." It is very difficult for a parent to watch a child "waste" his money. We work very hard to earn what we have, and we naturally do not like to see money "thrown away." But there are several points here. What is "something worthless"? Is there possibly some value to the child in being able to spend his money "any old way" he likes? How does a child learn to handle money responsibly?

Needless to say, an object may have value to a child that his parents cannot see. It may have value to a child even though he loses interest in it after a short time. Parents tend to think that longevity is all-important in a toy, practicality in clothes, but young people may think differently.

When a child spends all his allowance on the day he receives it and has nothing for the rest of the week, what does he do? Does he ask for an advance, swipe change from the dresser, or offer to do some chores to earn money? Does he moan about his fate, or contentedly accept his paupered condition until allowance day rolls around again? Allowing him to appreciate the consequences of his actions means refusing to advance him money if it is clear that he will only get deeper into debt. But giving him a chance to earn some is an honorable solution.

One idea on squandering money: The urge to spend wildly cannot be indulged by most of us later in life because our tastes become too expensive, our budgets too restrictive, our heads too sensible. Only when they are young can children indulge themselves fully in quite this way, without guilt or worry, unless parents impose it. After a while, they learn that 50¢ spent on a toy car on Monday cannot buy baseball cards on Thursday. And sooner or later, because of their own needs and desires, they *want* to learn how to manage better. Then they become receptive to parental guidance.

One eleven-year-old was referred to as "the last of the big-time spenders" by his family because he always raced over to the shopping center to spend his allowance the minute he got it. When he received a fairly large sum for a birthday or other occasion, he invariably spent it all that very day.

But there came a morning when he soberly informed his parents that he had "saved" his allowance and bought something special with it. Since this was only 24 hours after he had received it, his parents needed a few seconds to realize what their child was saying. He had resisted his usual impulse to spend his money immediately and had waited *a whole day*, considering the expenditure, before making his purchase. He was reporting what was for him a victory. Fortunately, his parents had had a good night's sleep and had their wits about them at that moment, so they were able to value and applaud what was indeed an accomplishment for this particular child. It is with such victories as these that a person moves forward.

The Danger of Overemphasis

A child is likely to learn to be responsible about money if (1) he is allowed to decide how to spend his own money; (2) he is not made to feel guilty or stupid about how he spends it; (3) his parents advise him, but not too often or too critically; and (4) he is intelligent enough to learn from his experiences, which our children are if we allow them the opportunity.

Sometimes parents who talk about their child's not knowing the value of money are guilty of valuing money over other important things in life. Perhaps their child feels that they put too high a premium on materialistic things, and he needs to rebel against that. Or perhaps the parents are using money as a weapon with which to manage the child. People have all sorts of quirks and foibles about money. We will spend a lot on furnishing our home, for example, but feel guilty about leaving a single light bulb burning "unnecessarily." All this is relatively harmless until we try to impose our peculiarities on our children as rules of reason. If a mother grew up with little, she may be tight-fisted with money even though more is available now, or she may be particularly liberal, wanting to give her children things she did not have. In either case, her children will not grow up in the same atmosphere as she did and probably will not feel about money as she does.

When children use money or possessions to compete or show off, or when they talk a great deal about money and who has what, they may be reflecting their parents' attitudes. It is often a good idea for parents to reexamine their behavior in this regard. Is the message they are sending what they really want to communicate to their child?

Of course, the way a child this age spends his money is not entirely his own business. He cannot be allowed to buy things we consider dangerous to his health and safety. We have a right to insist, for example, that he cannot buy a motorcycle, because we think he is too young to ride one, or buy cigarettes, alcohol, or drugs. A family's rules about certain places being off limits, certain movies being forbidden apply no matter whose money is involved. But a child ought to be free to make his own decisions within the protective boundaries the family has set.

How Much Allowance?

It is impossible to say what a typical allowance ought to be for a young person of eleven to fourteen. Family resources differ, as do children's needs, and of course what is typical varies from neighborhood to neighborhood throughout the country. A parent needs to know what other children in the child's class or neighborhood are receiving and also what those allowances cover. Obviously if Billie-down-the-block has to pay his carfare to and from school out of his allowance, the amount does not seem as big as it did at first glance. We always hear that "everybody" gets more money than our child. To hear him tell it, the rest of the gang live like oriental potentates compared to him. There always *are* a few children who seem to have

money to throw around, but what do most of the youngsters get? If a child really has less, that is, if he goes to a school or lives in a section where all the youngsters have a great deal more than he has, parents do need to discuss this with him and not ignore the problem or slough it off.

What should an allowance cover? When a small child first begins to receive an allowance, around age five, it is usually a very small sum—a nickel, a dime, seldom more—just enough to give him the feeling of having money of his very own to buy candy, or put in the bubble-gum machine, or purchase a small toy at the five and ten. Very few children are willing or able to save a portion of this first small amount—even for a week—and parents usually do not expect it. It is not at all unusual for the entire sum to be spent the day it is received.

Later on, the amount is increased, but it usually continues to cover only small personal pleasures, that is, candy, games, toys, and such. By the time they reach eleven or twelve, however, many children crave to handle larger sums of money and begin to have more definite opinions about how money spent on them should be used. Parents usually begin gradually to increase the child's allowance to cover other expenses. Movies, concerts, and similar entertainment are usually among the first items included. A child learns to save for such events and, since going to them is optional, he will not be deprived of any necessities of life while he is learning about budgeting his money satisfyingly.

If a child is managing well, parents can begin to include items such as writing paper, school supplies, transportation, hobbies, books, cosmetic and toilet items, gifts, after-school snacks, and minor articles of clothing. He must learn how to put aside the money for these items until he needs to make the purchases.

A girl who has shown good taste and judgment when shopping with her mother for clothes may now be given money to budget for certain items in her wardrobe. Underwear, socks, pajamas or nightgowns, and hair ribbons are a good beginning; mistakes in these are not crucial. Usually a parent does not increase a child's responsibilities in this way unless the child herself is anxious for it and has been or is now given certain preparation.

It is not enough for a parent simply to give a child a larger allowance and then leave her on her own. Parent and child need to consider how many pairs of socks, underwear, etc., the parents would ordinarily buy for the girl. Starting with a year's supply is often too difficult at the beginning. If it seems feasible, using a three-month period, or a season of the year, perhaps, is a comfortable way to begin. Then parent and child can begin to comparison-shop among stores and brands, go shopping together and get an idea of what these items generally cost, survey quality, size, color, available assortment.

A girl sees that if she splurges on one beautiful nightgown, she will be able to afford only three night-gowns instead of four. A parent's guidance includes pointing out this fact, and which materials shrink, and that the ribbons on the expensive nightgown will look less lovely after one washing because they need ironing and mother does not iron underwear and nightclothes.

The child sees that planning purchases requires thought, time, and effort. After considering the information, she makes her own choice. Over a period of time she will learn to take advantage of sales, to understand what is and is not a bargain, to get the most for her money. With experience, she will become more able and efficient.

Allow a Little Leeway

Including several categories of purchases in her allowance also gives a child a little leeway to be extravagant in one area if she is willing to economize in another. Needless to say, we expect mistakes at the start and do not overemphasize them. Later on we will be pleased as our thirteen-year-old picks up a blouse on a shopping trip, feels the material, and says knowingly, "This material is *cool* but it will look positively *gross* after a few washings." Just because a child has a clothing allowance does not mean that we cannot go along when a child buys. But we go only if wanted after the orientation days; that is the understanding.

With boys a more inclusive allowance usually does not begin with clothes; even the most clothes-conscious of today's Prince Valiants do not want to be bothered shopping for things to wear until they are older. They hate trying on and usually have neither the patience nor the interest for comparison-shopping. But they have other needs: sports equipment, hobbies, gifts for friends, clothing extras such as fancy belts or sporty shoes. The idea is to start with the item with which the child is most likely to succeed. Boys gain early a feeling for what constitutes a good bat, ball, and glove, for example, and are interested enough to learn to make sound judgments about purchasing them.

A child might be given a special sum of money earmarked for certain expenses only; or that sum can be pooled with his regular allowance, with the understanding that he must now pay for certain new expenses. In the first case, one does not run the risk that clothing money will be used for after-school snacks, and it is often a good way to begin. But after a while, one wants to move on to the next arrangement. When mistakes and imperfections are taken for granted in a family as part of the normal order of things, it is assumed that managing money, like everything else, will bring its share of error. Starting with small sums and fairly simple optional items decreases the risk.

We let our child know exactly what his allowance covers. We check with him every so often to see how things are going and to find out if he has some ideas about changes. But we do not hang over his shoulder. It is not unreasonable to ask for a rough accounting for the first few "pay days" after we have enlarged his allowance and responsibilities. But after that, a youngster should be free to keep his own counsel, unless we have reason to believe something is seriously wrong.

A few children are ready by the time they are almost fifteen to receive a "full" allowance that covers all their expenses, but most have not yet the experience or the judgment this requires and do not seek the added responsibility. But beginning at eleven, say, to increase the items covered by a child's allowance and gradually build his ability to manage his affairs over these years can have great advantages for a family.

Responsibility Helps

Parents and children tend to have many arguments about money during the adolescent years, and the more responsibility a child has for his own expenditures, the more reasonable he will be—probably—in his requests. Also, when parents make periodic reevaluations of his income, this cuts down on what can turn into frequent bickering over a multitude of items. If parents are fairly consistent and firm and refuse to be badgered into giving extra money except under extraordinary conditions, they avoid constant nagging, which occurs only if parents encourage it by rewarding it. We need to bend when there is a genuine financial emergency, but when pleading becomes routine we are free to suggest that the child start putting his own money away.

Taking on full responsibility for his financial affairs decreases a child's feeling of dependence upon his parents, a feeling that becomes increasingly onerous as he gets older. He begins to get the feeling that he can manage his own life, which makes him more optimistic about his future. He feels more important.

In our society we prolong the adolescent period by the lengthy schooling we expect of our young people. We live in an age when people tend to define themselves by the work they do: I'm a lawyer, or I'm an electrician, or whatever. But we have a large pariah group, the young, who are denied the opportunity to support themselves through productive work and must depend upon their parents for the basics of their lives for a very long preparatory period. Many of today's school dropouts reflect a need to begin ordering their own lives.

Giving a child a "full" allowance does not make him less financially dependent on us, but it does change the day-to-day basis on which he lives. He is buying and choosing his own clothes and accessories, his toilet articles, everything that can possibly be arranged under his aegis. As he gets older he will probably be expected to work in his spare time, to contribute toward these expenses. What is asked of him will depend on the working capability of the young person, the job opportunities in his area, and the financial situation of the family, plus his schoolwork load or other responsibilities such as music lessons or athletic practice. If a child is deeply involved with piano studies, for example, and practices for several hours a day, his family probably will not require a financial contribution from him unless they must.

It is a good idea to have periodic reviews with a child of how he is coming along. If he never has any money and cannot figure out where it has gone (a not uncommon complaint of adults as well as children), he ought to try keeping a record of what he spends. If this seems a terrible burden, he can regard it as a temporary measure only, to be done for several weeks or a month until he gets a clearer picture of his spending. Although a child should be free enough to make mistakes in spending, he ought to know what the mistakes are so that he can learn from them.

Permitting a child to use his own judgment does not mean that a parent withdraws entirely. As with other things, first we do it for them, then with them, then they do it while we watch, then they go it alone with guidance as needed.

10

Drugs
And Other
Escape Mechanisms

CHILDREN DO NOT, at first, ask sophisticated questions about drugs. They want to know the answer to one very simple question: "Why—if heroin and LSD and drugs like that are so dangerous—do people take them?" A very sensible question. But the answer is not easy. Because if people did not derive certain pleasures from these drugs there would be no problem. Nobody would use them.

The child, searching to unravel the mystery, persists: "Why do people use drugs?" (He is not, of course, talking about drugs prescribed for illness.) It is tempting to make the answer as simple and straightforward as the question. After all, we feel, drugs *are* bad; we do not want our children anywhere near them. So we may respond that anybody who smokes marijuana, shoots heroin, takes pills is sick, or bad, or crazy. "Drugs are poison, you must have nothing to do with them. You can see for yourself in the newspapers that people are dying every day from breaking that rule." Simple, really.

But it isn't. Now that we are some years into the drug scene we should know that if the problem were that easily handled, more and more children would not be involved with drugs of a dozen different descriptions. Why can't we simplify our response? Because any such simplified warning is not true and, because of that, it is not going to send us home free. The very first time our child sees a perfectly normal friend contentedly puffing a joint of marijuana—and offering him one—it is going to be very clear that we lied to him on at least one score. This picture will be so different from the sick scene we painted that he may wonder if any part of our warning against drugs is true. In lumping all drugs and drug users together, we have made it possible that our child will use them also once he sees the kid next door or the gang at school smoking marijuana with apparent safety; he may assume that the whole drug scene is as harmless as this looks to him. Of course, such an assumption is untrue. Even marijuana smoking is *not* without danger. But we are not in a good position to convince him of the possible dangers if we ourselves have thrown everything into the same bag and colored it an unrelieved, macabre black.

Answering First Questions

What then do we do with that first question? Of course, a single pointed question does not appear out of the blue one fine day to be dealt with honestly and intelligently once and for all. As with imparting information about sex, we give our children the facts about drugs over a long period of time. The drug scene comes to their attention at an early age now. Probably we have already had some discussions about it with our child. But as he gets older he will hear about drugs and see people using them. Chances are he will be approached to try them, probably by a friend. He will need to talk about the various drugs again and again. He will be talking about this with friends. He should also be talking with us. He will need to receive increasingly sophisticated answers with more and more information in response to his questions.

Very few of us are well prepared for this job. Heroin, marijuana, LSD, "speed" (methedrine or methamphetamine), and the rest were probably not in our experience as children or young adults. Now we must learn what dangers—and attractions—they hold for our children. The latter—attractions—is where a lot of us get hung up. We have a bright, curious eleven-year-old boy, alive to life and its possibilities. And he asks that question: "Why?" We find that we have tremendous difficulty admitting to him the very simple, obvious fact that people take drugs to make them feel good, to give them feelings and sensations that are intensely pleasurable, interesting, exciting. Or give freedom from pain, both physical and emotional, relieve tension and anxiety. Or to impart a feeling of being at peace with oneself and one's surroundings.

Says singer (and former speed freak) Johnny Cash:

I'll tell you why I took amphetamines, because it felt good. There isn't anybody can get a kid off drugs by telling him it doesn't feel good. He knows how it makes him feel. For a while you're so stimulated, your mind is like a high-speed camera clicking away at three hundred and sixty degrees and you see and know everything. There are all those beautiful visions, all right, and those realizations and feelings of love and awareness.

But we dare not tell this to that curious, questing young person. We are frightened that once he knows this secret he will want to experiment for himself. Everything in his environment impels him to seek a good feeling. In the words of one young person, "It's a good thing to feel good, and the sooner you feel gooder the better."

But *we* know the secret and *we* are not seduced into using such drugs. Why? Because we also know the very grave dangers involved, and we are not willing to take the risk. For most of us, in effect, the game is not worth the candle. Says Johnny Cash:

You go down the other side of that whole thing, and the going down ain't worth the coming up. . . . I still worry that I might have damaged my brain with pills. I don't think so, but I'll tell you, even after three years off drugs, at least once a week I'll have a horrible nightmare. I've got pills in my pocket that I'm trying to hide from somebody, and I'm always falling down and cursing myself, and somebody's chasing me and I'm going to jail, and somebody's beating me. All kinds of horrible things. At least once a week. It was every night at first.

The Need for Trust

But our children do not have our experience, our judgment. Can we trust them? There comes a point in every youngster's life when that question becomes irrelevant; unless we are going to put a 24-hour guard on him, we must trust him. But, we may still protest, at this age wouldn't we be justified in shading the truth a little to protect him a while longer? Why should we open the door?

We must face the fact that the door is already open. If we want to be believed later, we must be honest now. We even have to try not to make mistakes out of ignorance, because children tend to believe that such mistakes are intentional distortions.

We do not, however, just throw a book labeled "drug facts" at our child and let him loose with it, any more than we do with information about sex. We tell him what he asks or needs to know, and along with this we impart our own value judgments and our feelings about how we hope he will act. His protection, then, comes from a combination of his own intelligence and judgment and what he is able to take from us.

As we go along, we will want to tell him the complete truth, offering as much scientific detail as he can handle about what the various drugs are, what they do, how they affect one's thinking, feeling, and behavior, their dangers and their pleasures and the special hazards they present for young users. Our child will seek to understand the differences between the various drugs and, as time passes, will probably begin to ask increasingly complex questions, both philosophical and provocative: Why not get high once in a while? Does marijuana make a person feel sexy? Why do you smoke or drink (if you do) when cigarettes can cause cancer and alcohol can lead to alcoholism? When we know the answer, we should tell him what we know. If we feel unsure of our facts, we ought to say so and try to inform ourselves more adequately. If our child questions our own use of drugs—alcohol, tobacco, sleeping pills, etc.—we need to avoid reacting defensively. Admitting our fallibility is less damaging to our standing with him than arguing the point. The child is usually more interested in communicating honestly than in faulting us.

Here are some of the basic facts about the most common drugs used and abused today.

Heroin

Heroin, also called smack, horse, H, and scag, is not a controversial drug. Derived from opium, it kills the pains of the body, the pains of the mind, and, quite often, the user himself. Why would anyone want to try heroin? When injected into a vein it produces a "rush" of excitement that is sometimes described as akin to sexual orgasm. Within a few minutes, the person begins to feel drowsy; he feels pleasantly warm and at peace with himself and the world; he feels self-confident, like "somebody." For persons who have difficulty experiencing these feelings in everyday living, the drug exerts a powerful attraction.

Unfortunately, when the drug wears off, reality with all its pain returns. In order to continue to escape, the user continues to take the drug. But he must take it in increasing amounts because his body begins quickly to build up a "tolerance" to it; he needs more and more heroin to achieve the same effect. Soon he may need to have it three or four times a day. In a very short time the user's previous worries are replaced by one all-consuming preoccupation—where he is going to get his next "fix." At this point, the main reason for using the drug is to avoid the misery of not having it. The drug experience has become the purpose of his life. He has become "addicted"; that is, he suffers severe "withdrawal" symptoms if his body is deprived of the drug.

Youngsters often begin by sniffing heroin, usually under the mistaken belief that this is not dangerous. However, heroin passes quickly through the nasal membranes into the bloodstream, and one can become addicted, or die, from sniffing as well as from injecting. The progression to injecting heroin under the skin ("skin popping") and finally into a vein ("mainlining") occurs as the user is drawn by his need for a stronger and faster "fix." Becoming listless and apathetic, he is often unable to maintain a regular school schedule at this point or to sustain genuine relationships with others. In addition, large sums of money are required to support a "habit," so that the addict must frequently resort to stealing—sometimes from his family—or other criminal activity.

Heroin addicts suffer from a variety of physical ailments directly related to their habit: abscesses, collapsed veins, and infection from unsterile syringes or needles are common, as is hepatitis, spread through shared needles. Preoccupied with the search for heroin and indifferent to food, users become generally run-down and are easy prey to infections. Tuberculosis and pneumonia are not uncommon. When drugged they are less sensitive to pain; they may injure themselves and not know it. Deaths from overdose ("OD") are reported daily. In New York City, heroin kills more young people than all the contagious diseases combined.

Most youngsters, if fully informed of the dangers of this narcotic, will not experiment with it, understanding that heroin is not a joyride to be taken casually now and then to brighten a dull Sunday. Those who get into heroin are often children with a strong need to flirt with danger, a need to hurt themselves or their parents, or those who find life too hard to bear and cannot resist the temporary escape provided by the drug experience. They often have a greater than average sense of incompetence and do not experience excitement in their daily lives. They assume the future holds only failure for them, and look toward a tomorrow in which things are going to get worse.

LSD

LSD (lysergic acid diethylamide, "acid") is a man-made chemical so powerful that approximately 150,000th of an ounce is a sufficient dose for one person for several hours. Colorless, odorless, and tasteless, it is ordinarily sold either in a sugar cube in which a tiny drop of LSD has been absorbed, in powder form, or in capsules of various colors.

Why do people take LSD? They experience hallucinations (sensory experiences not caused by external stimuli) of sight and sound and, to a lesser extent, of taste, smell, and touch. Walls may appear to move, colors seem more brilliant, unusual patterns appear, music can be "seen" as well as heard, time slows down or seems to go in reverse. Images appear, sometimes realistic, sometimes fantastic. LSD "trips" come on within a half hour or more after taking the drug, are most vivid in about two hours, and continue for varying periods of time up to perhaps 10 to 16 hours, gradually diminishing.

Users often feel more creative (although studies to compare creativity before and after LSD experiences have found no significant changes) and have a sense of oneness with the universe and of gaining insights into their own personalities. The experience is strongly emotional, often visionary and dreamlike.

The Bad Trip

Frequently, however, the dream is a nightmare, a "bad trip," with feelings of dread and horror that may include sensations that one's body is dissolving and that one is losing one's mind. Although LSD is not known to be addictive, there are many cases on record of the development of psychosis and severe and lasting anxiety or depression after an acid trip. Strangely, too, there occur "flashbacks"—a recurrence of the LSD experience days or even months after the drug was last taken. These may be brought on by physical or emotional stress, by smoking marijuana, or by taking certain medications, and they can be intensely frightening.

The kind of experience a person has with LSD can vary greatly depending upon his personality, his mood at the time, the people with him, and the circumstances in which the drug is taken. The same dose may act differently upon the same person at two different times, or it may produce both ecstasy and horror during one trip. Certain personality types find it particularly difficult to tolerate the alterations of feelings that occur under the influence of the drug. Crippling and death by accident are possible also; persons feeling they can float or fly may step out of high windows or, feeling invincible, may walk into a lane of moving traffic.

Some studies have purported to show that women who have taken LSD during early pregnancy or shortly before conception run a higher risk of giving birth to abnormal babies. These studies have now been discredited. There is some indication that repeated use of LSD may cause lasting chromosomal damage to the user, but the evidence is inconclusive. Clearly, however, any substance whose effects are so powerful and unpredictable is dangerous.

Several other substances produce effects similar to LSD, although milder. The two most widely known are mescaline, which comes from the peyote cactus, and psilosybin, which comes from the Mexican "sacred mushroom."

Stimulants and Depressants

Stimulants and depressants come in pills of many colors and are designed to change one's mood upon demand. Want to fly? Take a pretty orange pill. Want to cool it? Take a "red bird" or a "yellow jacket." These "up" and "down" drugs have been with us for a long time. Because of our familiarity with them and because they have legitimate medical uses, many parents tend to be unduly casual about them.

Young people take "up" drugs in order to reduce

fatigue, increase their alertness, and achieve a feeling of well-being. Amphetamines such as Benzedrine and Dexedrine ("Bennies" and "Dexies") are used to help them cram for an examination, to have more energy for athletics, or to stay awake in order to drive. Or they may take an "up" because they're feeling down. Because these drugs also suppress the appetite, they are used in dieting as well. "Up" drugs also include cocaine, which is being used more and more frequently, caffeine, and nicotine.

What are the dangers? If you don't *feel* hungry or tired—even though you lack food and sleep—you may push yourself further than is good for you, perhaps going without food or sleep for several days. In addition, when the drug wears off, you will tend to feel the accumulated fatigue and be depressed. The temptation, then, is to take more pills, falling into an insidious cycle that is difficult to break. People who get into the habit of using stimulants to pull them out of the doldrums usually lose weight, become jumpy and irritable, and are often suspicious and hostile. They become run down and are less resistant to infection. Heavy doses may cause a temporary psychosis, involving feelings of terror, confusion, and loss of touch with reality. Abrupt withdrawal of the drug from a heavy user can result in a deep and suicidal depression.

Another "up" drug, Methedrine ("speed"), is sometimes injected intravenously to produce a "rush," a feeling of intense exhilaration.

This "rush" ebbs within minutes and is followed by a high, a flood of physical and mental energy, a feeling of power. The thoughts of the "speed freak" may

run faster than his ability to articulate them, so that his speech is often unintelligible to someone not tuned into his wavelength. When the drug wears off, in two to four hours, the user feels weak, exhausted and, again, down.

The dangers associated with using other stimulants are present with Methedrine, only more so. The user often becomes irrational, impulsive, and sometimes violent. There is a progressive deterioration of his relationships with family and friends and of his normal inhibitions. He becomes run down and is easy prey to infection. He often suffers from abscesses, collapsed veins, and related problems that any person who injects a drug intravenously is subject to. Liver damage may result. Occasionally, death during athletic contests has

been blamed on the use of speed or other amphetamines. It is probably more accurate to view the drug as
contributing to death from other causes. Young people
who are into the drug scene warn that "speed kills."

The pace of life has led many adults to turn to
"down" drugs—barbiturates, tranquilizers, and alcohol
—in order to relax from the tensions of their existence.
Young people often find these drugs first in their own
homes and use—and abuse—them for the same purpose
their parents do. Barbiturates (Seconal, Nembutal, and
phenobarbital) and tranquilizers (Miltown, Equanil,
and Librium) calm a person down and help him sleep.
When they are used often, tolerance develops—one
needs more to produce the same effect—and the user
can become addicted to and dependent upon them.
With heavy users, withdrawal of the drug requires hos-
pitalization. Deaths from overdose can occur. Combina-
tions of drugs such as barbiturates with alcohol can
be especially lethal.

Alcohol

Alcohol (ethyl alcohol) is well known enough not
to require extensive discussion here. Roughly 70,000,000
Americans drink with some regularity, ranging from
small amounts to overindulgence. They drink seeking
relaxation, self-confidence, an escape from unpleasant
reality, an aid to sociability, or, simply, pleasure.

Many people believe that alcohol is a stimulant
because it does provide an initial lift. But this sense
of well-being comes because one's aches and pains and
worries are depressed. One's inhibitions and controls
are depressed, too, so that people find the "nerve" to

do things they would not—and sometimes should not—
do if they were not under the influence of alcohol. Most
adults who drink are able to enjoy their liquor in moderation and lead perfectly normal lives. But according to
the National Institute of Mental Health, an estimated
5,000,000 to 6,000,000 adults in the United States are
alcoholics and perhaps 10 per cent of all drinkers cause
serious personal problems to themselves and their families by their drinking. In addition, alcohol, because it
depresses their reflexes, impairs their ability to drive a
car. It does not, however, always discourage people
from driving, and half of all fatal crashes involve drinking drivers. There is, in addition, abundant testimony
linking excessive drinking with arrests for crime. Alcohol is addictive.

Writing ten years ago in *The Intelligent Parents'
Guide to Teen-agers*, Thelma C. Purtell said:

The use of alcohol is apparently incorporated in
our adolescent culture whether we like to face the
fact or not. In a society that accepts adult drinking,
it is natural that teen-agers, in making demands
for adult prerogatives, should include the right to
find out for themselves about liquor as well as
everything else. Drinking by the teen-ager, beyond
the family circle, constitutes another form of experimentation in the business of becoming an
adult. The amazing thing is that this can occur in
a nation which through its laws makes clear that
young people are not expected to drink at all.

Mrs. Purtell also said, "Parents will have solved

the drinking problem when they have helped their young people to be the sort of individuals who do not need to turn to such a treacherous ally in times of boredom, anxiety, or adversity." Now, a decade later, much the same words of advice are being offered to parents concerned about their children's interest in other drugs, and alcohol continues to be a problem.

Today, Peter Marin and Allan Y. Cohen write, "Drugs (meaning marijuana et al.) have become . . . a normal part of the adolescent world."

Marijuana

Marijuana (pot, tea, grass, or dope) is derived from the common hemp plant, *Cannabis sativa*, and is commonly smoked in pipes or cigarettes called reefers or joints. But it is more than a drug. It has become a symbol of today's youth culture. Feelings about marijuana often serve to distinguish the young from the old, and to alienate the young from the old. There is great controversy about marijuana, and it has become difficult to separate fact from myth. Respected physicians differ in their interpretations of the available data and in their views about the possibilities of danger from prolonged or heavy use. Because of the highly emotional climate that surrounds the drug and because of the variability of its effects on different users and under different circumstances, it is difficult for parents to make a judgment about it.

One fact, though, is clear. Huge numbers of young people are experimenting with marijuana today, and before our children are very much older they will be forced to make a decision about whether or not to try it themselves. We ought to think back and remember how many of us took our first sip of alcohol or first puff of a cigarette—whose taste and effects we may have found unpleasant—because of pressure to do what everyone else was doing or to appear sophisticated to our friends. There is similar pressure on our children today to try marijuana. A child may be curious to see for himself what it is like, or he may want to be able to say he's tried it, or he doesn't want to have to say he hasn't tried it. So we must attempt to understand what it is, what it offers to the young, and what dangers it may hold for them. Then we can decide how to discuss the problem with our children.

Varying Effects

What is it like to smoke marijuana? This question cannot be answered simply. The quality of the drug is not constant; the chemical potency of the hemp plant can vary greatly, and the purity of a particular reefer is always in question because marijuana is distributed illegally—you can't be sure what you're getting. Sometimes it is mixed with other drugs or substances that may be dangerous. In addition, the same amount of marijuana of a particular quality can have different effects upon different persons—and indeed upon the same person at different times. A great deal depends on the "set"—whom you are with, where you are, how you are feeling. Are you relaxed, happy, unpressured? Or are you ill at ease, tired, apprehensive? Are you with friends you like and can trust? Or are you alone or in uncongenial surroundings? Marijuana will tend to accentuate the existing conditions, so that you feel more relaxed, or more anxious, depending upon how you felt to start with.

In ordinary low doses, marijuana usually produces a mild euphoria. Immediate physical effects usually include a reddening of the whites of the eyes, an increased heart rate, dryness of the mouth and throat, and a cough owing to the irritating effect of the smoke on the lungs. At the start of a "high" many smokers giggle as if at a private joke, then become quiet and reflective. Most users report experiencing a heightened perception of their surroundings; their appreciation of people, objects, and various activities is enhanced. They say they see colors and shapes more vividly, that listening to music gives more pleasure and yields new sensations. Time is slowed down. One may seem to exist outside the passage of time much as one does while daydreaming. The marijuana smoker tends to focus on himself and his experience and prefers to ponder rather than to act. He feels pleasantly warm, at peace with the world. He rarely becomes aggressive or domineering, in contrast to a person intoxicated with alcohol. Marijuana is not a narcotic and is not addictive. No physical craving develops for it, and it causes no hangover.

Most smokers of marijuana use it occasionally, perhaps a reefer no more (and probably less) than once a week. They continue to function in school and at work. They use it as a means of relaxing, to be employed with discrimination. Sociologist Enrich Goode writes, in *The Marijuana Smokers*:

The recreational character of pot smoking is possibly its most outstanding feature. A typical intimate, informal (four to ten people) pot party will involve frequently and typically passing the joint from person to person and staring into space for long stretches of time with nothing apparently actually going on. . . . It will appear boring and vacuous to someone who is not high . . . the marijuana experience is typically thought of as *itself* a recreation. Being high is thought of as fun, a state of pleasure. For one who is not high and never has been, understanding its appeal, especially at such a party, would be like sitting in a concert hall and being deaf.

What are the dangers of marijuana smoking? As long as the use of marijuana is illegal, there is a danger of obtaining marijuana that has been contaminated by some other substance. The immediate source may be a friend, but there is no way of knowing the road the marijuana traveled before it reached him. Some young people have had severe reactions to marijuana; hallucinations and short spells of terror and paranoia have been reported. Whether this was because of contamination or the personality of the user is not entirely clear.

We do not yet know enough about the physical and psychological effects of long-term use of marijuana. A large number of studies, by both private and government agencies, are being conducted to determine the answers to these questions. Meanwhile, we cannot say with certainty that even moderate use over a number of years is without risks.

Marijuana can trigger the return of symptoms, including hallucinations, of an earlier LSD trip.

While under the influence of marijuana, the user may have lapses of immediate memory; he may forget what he has just said or done and have difficulty in judging distances. Since marijuana also alters his perception of time, it is clearly a hazard in driving a car. Most smokers, however, have no urge to drive while high on marijuana. Perception returns to normal when the effects of the drug wear off.

Excessive Use of Marijuana

Some young people become heavily involved with marijuana. The marijuana experience becomes the most important thing in their lives and they spend a good deal of time arranging it and discussing it. They tend to lose interest in school, other activities, and "straight" friends. Obviously, for them the drug is a hazard.

Excessive marijuana use, like excessive drinking, is an indication of other adolescent difficulties. Although marijuana is the means the child uses to "tune out," one needs to learn what problems in his life make prolonged escape so appealing.

Most experts are careful to distinguish between the use of marijuana by adolescents and by adults. This is important to keep in mind. Research bears out the fact that all drugs are most potentially dangerous and unpredictable in their effect if the user is of unstable personality. And adolescence is a time when under normal circumstances the personality is unstable. The staff of the Child Study Association writes:

When marijuana is used as an easy way out of anxiety, restlessness, self-questioning—troubles traditionally associated with adolescence—development may be slowed down or postponed indefinitely. The task of growing up cannot be accomplished without a certain amount of struggle and pain. It is by fighting through his problems as they occur that an adolescent learns who he is and builds strengths to cope with the inevitable stresses of later life. Although a young person may argue that drugs are "where it's at," their use can make it impossible for the user to know truly where he's at in his emotional development.

Parents and children need to be concerned with the fact that use or possession of marijuana is still in many states a crime for which young people are being sent to jail, sometimes for long terms. Is this a risk a young person wants to take? A police record is a serious matter.

Marijuana and Sex
Does marijuana increase the pleasures of sex or make a young person sexually promiscuous? Boys in particular are often drawn to drugs by their fears of sexual inadequacy and the hope of finding an aphrodisiac that will give them confidence, courage, or magic powers to heighten their own or a partner's pleasure in sex.

Of course, in this age of relaxed sexual mores, parents (and many adolescents) are frightened by any possibility that standards may be lowered through use of a drug. In *Drugs and Youth*, Dr. Robert Coles, Dr. Joseph H. Brenner, and Dermot Meagher write:

The use of marijuana does not lead in itself to promiscuity or to sexual liaisons that may be later regretted. The actual effects of marijuana on sexual desire, arousal and performance are usually related quite directly to the sexual maturity and experiential knowledge of the user. Young persons who have not yet had sexual intercourse are not likely to be aroused by marijuana; in fact, if anything, many related that in this respect grass turns them off. On the other hand, some who have enjoyed a steady sexual relationship with one partner have asserted that, after smoking marijuana and often for a day or two afterwards, the act of sexual intercourse becomes much more stimulating and satisfying. They claim to enjoy a fresh excitement and a new delight in their own and their partner's body.

Does marijuana lead invariably to the use of heroin or other such strong drugs? This belief arose because it was found that many heroin addicts had smoked marijuana before trying heroin. However, even more heroin addicts have drunk alcohol before going on to heroin. The kind of person who is drawn to that long road will probably try several drugs along the way. But neither alcohol nor marijuana sets him on a course that heads inevitably (or even usually) to heroin. It has been remarked that the use of marijuana puts a person on the "drug scene" where heroin is also available, at the same time lowering his inhibitions so that he might be drawn into using a drug that he would otherwise resist. Nevertheless, the fact remains that the overwhelming number of marijuana smokers do *not* go on to heroin.

Psychological Dependence

Is marijuana habit forming (habituating)? Yes, although it is not physically addictive. Like other habits, it can be broken—with more or less difficulty, more or less regret, depending upon the psychological need it fills for the user. However, withdrawal is not accompanied by physical symptoms.

There is often confusion about the terms habituation, dependence, and addiction. Coles, Brenner, and Meagher point out that all of us are creatures of habit; we are habituated to eating at certain times, combing our hair a certain way, and adhering to innumerable other routines in the course of a day. Some habits we think of as good, others as bad.

The repetitive act of taking a favorite drink every day is a habit . . . to do without it could be felt as deprivation. But when there is no dependence or craving, it is a simple habit, albeit one not willingly given up.

What differentiates dependence from habit? When a person depends on something or someone it is implied that without that support he would suffer a state of disequilibrium. He might or might not be able to take steps to restore his equilibrium by shifting dependence to another direction or by readjusting his needs.

Psychological dependence on drugs can create

special problems for adolescents who, as we have noted, are particularly vulnerable to drug use because of their immaturity. Parents are understandably concerned about experimentation with marijuana. They fear that their youngsters might become seduced into smoking on a regular basis. This depends upon the individual. Some young people with serious problems have a greater need to escape from everyday pressures than others. But Dr. Coles and many other professionals say that the excitement of smoking pot is not so seductive to the more solid young people. They can take it or leave it. They find it interesting but not so enticing that they would be likely to become overinvolved with it. It is like alcohol. Of the many individuals who try alcohol, those who become alcoholics are the ones who have other problems.

Of the great number of adolescents and young adults who smoke marijuana, only a very small percentage become psychologically dependent on it. Admittedly, these few are indeed in trouble. The dependence, however, is determined much more by the particular drabness, pain and ugliness of their lives and of the immediate world in which they live than by the actual smoking of marijuana in whatever quantity.

Psychological dependence is not the same as addiction. Marijuana, unlike heroin and some other drugs, is not addictive. Addiction to a drug takes place when profound changes occur in the chemistry and physiology, or the workings, of the body—profound, but reversible changes . . . Near normal bodily functions can go on only when a continual supply of the drug is pumped into the system . . . The person who is addicted suffers painful withdrawal symptoms if the supply of the addictive drug is stopped abruptly. For example, a chronic alcoholic, upon withdrawal, may "go into the DTs" (delirium tremens) with convulsions, hallucinations and feelings of terror; the person addicted to barbiturates . . . will suffer severe irritability and insomnia, possibly accompanied by convulsions seven to ten days after withdrawal. Fortunately, the withdrawal symptoms can be greatly modified and danger diminished with good medical care. It is clear that the chemical system of the body takes an appreciable time to adjust to functioning without the addictive drug.

Our Children and Drugs

Having achieved a certain understanding of the effects of the more commonly used (and abused) drugs, and the differences among them, a parent is better prepared to think clearly about the threat they may possibly pose to his or her own individual child. What are our expectations? Do we expect our child not to experiment with any drugs whatsoever—ever? Or do we view the problem as involving a number of factors, such as the nature of a particular drug, the age and nature of the user, the frequency of use? Are these expectations realistic in terms of the kind of child our youngster is, his friends, his school, his general environment? Where expectations are unrealistic, they deprive a child of useful guidelines.

Many parents in the past tried to make sure their children would never smoke a cigarette or take a drink. They felt they had legitimate reasons for this position. But is it reasonable to expect that a child will never try what his friends try if he feels he is stable, his friends say it's great, and his friends aren't all bad? What happens to parent-child communication when youngsters feel their parents have a closed mind on any subject?

Of course, conditions vary in different sections of the country. However, in many areas today parents should be prepared for the probability that their high school child will try marijuana at least once. Considering the availability of marijuana, its appeal to the young, and the fact that its dangers are often equated by responsible persons with those of alcohol (which many parents drink), a normal child is likely to be highly curious about it. Many factors will affect how he handles his curiosity. Is he very much influenced by what other children do? Does he always have to wear what the others wear, get the same haircut, and so on? Then he will probably be more likely to go along with his peers in experimenting with drugs, also. Is he inclined to be independent, to think things through on his own, to resist group pressure? His reaction may be different.

Keeping the Lines Open

If we accept the possibility that a child might want to try marijuana, we make it possible for him to continue to communicate with us no matter what happens. If we refuse to entertain this possibility the child may try it anyway but then have only his friends to discuss the situation with. How do we make it plain to a child that we are against certain behavior and at the same time create the kind of atmosphere in which our children feel they can come to us with any concerns or problems they may have? This is similar to the way parents convey their values about sex. When we ourselves were growing up, many parents did not want to sanction premarital sex but wished to be available if a girl did get into difficulty. Some parents were able to meet this difficult challenge admirably, but others created such fear that if their child got into trouble she was desperately afraid to go to her parents and thus lost the benefit of their advice and support.

Now, although we may recognize the possibility of our child's wanting to discover for himself what marijuana is like, we are justified in hoping that he will not experiment with it at this age, just as we would feel very differently about his having sexual relations at thirteen than at eighteen or twenty. Parents are on reasonable ground in wanting children to postpone certain experiences until they reach a certain age. A thirteen-year-old cannot handle an altered emotional state comfortably; one would not want a thirteen-year-old to drink a whole highball. In addition, he has not the judgment to make a good decision about whether to repeat the experience.

Parents often let a child have a sip of alcohol or glass of wine as he gets older, so that he can satisfy his curiosity about this drug at home, rather than elsewhere. But marijuana, of course, is illegal. It is foolish for a parent to break the law and smoke pot with a child. That is not the kind of message we want to get across.

At this age, one might say, "You know there are many things, like driving a car, that you have to wait to do until you're old enough. I don't think you are old enough to experiment with any drug right now. I hope you will wait and decide what to do about this when you're more experienced." We give our reasons for believing that age does make a difference in this case. We also assume that, as with limits about other issues, when our child is mature enough, he will make his own decisions.

In communicating our knowledge and values and expectations, the necessity for absolute honesty and avoidance of scare tactics cannot be overstressed. One mother reported watching with her eleven-year-old boy a television documentary that showed a young drug user

having his stomach pumped after an overdose of barbiturates. "You can imagine how much it must hurt to
have those tubes put down your throat," she remarked.

"No, it doesn't," he came back. "When you have
a lot of pills in you, you don't feel the pain." It is un-
fortunate, but children these days seem to expect their
parents not to level with them about drugs. When they
catch a parent in a mistake—intentional or not—or
even an exaggeration, their cynical expectations are con-
firmed. Needless to say, it lessens their trust.

How should we set forth our opinions about experimenting with drugs to our child—as hopes, recommendations, flat prohibitions? The way we discuss what
we expect of our child in this area ought to be consistent with our way of confronting other issues—it
should, in other words, fit into our overall relationship
with our child. Parents tend to become very panicky
and deal with the issue in a manner that is not characteristic of them. Out of fear, they may close their eyes
to the possibility that a problem might exist—thereby
seeming to their child to be more permissive than
they really are—or they may suddenly become rigidly
authoritarian.

Discuss Risk-Taking

At some point we might try to get into a discussion of taking risks in general. This is a topic that
nearly always interests children this age, and it is vitally
relevant to the drug scene. When a child buys a raffle
ticket, for example, he is avid to hear who the winner
is; maybe he will be one of the lucky ones, he thinks
excitedly. But when that same young person considers

the risks involved in experimenting with marijuana he may tend to minimize or dismiss the possibility that he could be one of the unlucky ones.

A child needs to learn to weigh the possible consequences—pro and con—of everything he would like to do. If he wanted to try marijuana, for example, what desirable effects might he expect? What are the chances of his achieving them, and how much does he want or need this? What are the drawbacks—physical, emotional, or if he gets into trouble at school or with the police? Would he be harming anyone else? What would happen if he did not try marijuana? Is the real risk sufficiently large so that the possible gain is just not worth it? When a child and a parent can discuss risk-taking rationally, the chances of a child's acting rashly are diminished. Children need help from their parents in learning how to weigh variables and make good decisions. But they are turned off by parents who tend to turn what starts out as honest discussion into a lecture.

Sooner or later most youngsters ask their parents, "How can you talk about a drug if you haven't had any experience with it?" Or, "Don't knock it if you haven't tried it." One should avoid being drawn into a debate, but we might point out that most of what we know we have not learned from personal experience but from the accumulated experience and study of others—scientific discoveries, historical facts. Unfortunately, young people, although they can appreciate this intellectually, often just are not satisfied by it. They suspect that our reaction to marijuana is partly emotional, caused by our lack of experience and fear of the unknown, more than by the hard facts. It never helps to argue about this.

We can make known the real risks entailed. Above all, we need to listen, hear what our child has to say, trying not to interrupt him even if we believe he is mistaken. If we can remain calm and really hear what our child is telling us, we can learn a lot about what is happening in his group and what he is confronted with—information he might not otherwise share with us. There is nothing to be gained from trying to argue him down.

Family Patterns Are Significant

Other aspects of family life may become involved in parent-child discussions of drugs as a child gets older. For example, what is the family's pattern of using drugs that are "socially acceptable"? Do they pop a pill for the slightest ache? Do they take sleeping pills or diet pills or tranquilizing pills frequently, or to excess? Do they preach about marijuana with a cigarette between their fingers? Do they need coffee to get them moving every morning and a few drinks to relax them every night?

Marin and Cohen write that some of "what appears to parents and the young as rebellion is in part an imitation of adults: a grotesque unconscious mimicking of their patterns of distraction and escape. The young continually see adults treating their own symptoms, changing their own moods. Adults rarely confront the underlying causes of their discomfort."

A study of 5,900 junior and senior high school students in Canada showed that students whose mothers used tranquilizers were three and a half times as likely to be on marijuana as the children of mothers who did not; five times as likely to be on LSD or amphetamines;

seven times as likely to be on tranquilizers; and ten times as likely to be on heroin or other opiates. Similarly a study of 12,000 students at six junior and senior high schools in New Jersey revealed that fathers of students who have injected speed used prescription tranquilizers or stimulants at a rate five and a half times that of the fathers of nonusers. Among mothers the rate was three times as high. Illicit drug use was shown to be two to three times as frequent among students whose parents smoked one or more packs of cigarettes as day as among students whose parents smoked less or not at all. No such relation was found in the case of parents who drank in moderation.

When children ask, "Why do you smoke when cigarettes make you more susceptible to cancer, heart disease, and other illnesses?" our answer may be instructive. Many adults started smoking before these dangers were well known and now find it difficult to stop even though they may want to.

When a young person asks, "Why do you drink when alcohol can lead to alcoholism?" the answer may be instructive to us as well as them. Alcohol was part of our experience as we grew up. Although most of us know at least one problem drinker, we see this as the exception rather than the rule and do not live in fear that drinking in moderation will lead to alcoholism. The Child Study Association of America writes:

> Those who use drugs in moderation do not have to be apologetic to their children and they are in the best position to respond effectively. Parents who depend heavily upon one or several drugs may be

in for a harder time. They are likely to feel guilty and defensive and consequently are handicapped in discussing drugs with their children. It does not help in such cases to argue that alcohol, cigarettes and tranquilizers are not illegal. What is important is that our children understand that we do not approve of excessive use of drugs by any age group or any person including ourselves.

When we are honest with our children and admit our fallibility, they respect us. Even parents who have had or still have extremely serious problems with drugs are not necessarily disqualified from providing the guidance their children need. It makes the task more difficult but not impossible. Very few young people are interested in condemning their parents for past errors; they are much more interested in a candid discussion about drugs in which their parents demonstrate their ability to look objectively at their own drug use.

The Allure of "Escape"

Drugs, of course, are not the only way people escape from the tensions of daily living. Nor are young people the only ones who seek escape. The pressures of marriage, child-rearing, unpaid bills, work—being alive—are such that everyone seeks to escape them periodically. We have our "escapist" literature and movies, entertainment that does not ask too much of us and takes our minds off our troubles temporarily. Mothers may escape the chores of the household by taking an afternoon off and doing as they please. If we didn't allow ourselves such releases occasionally, we wouldn't function as well. It isn't escape that's a bad idea. What is?

When a woman leaves a sinkful of dishes at home as she goes off on "an afternoon out," she will find the dishes there when she returns. When we leave our problems behind for a while they don't disappear, either. And we do not expect them to—we face them anew, perhaps refreshed, when we return. When any escape mechanism is used constantly to avoid dealing with problems that could and should be faced and worked through, it becomes destructive.

Young people, of course, particularly need to work through the problems of growing up and not avoid or postpone them. They, too, may use escape mechanisms other than drugs. Some have an overactive social life. Others, like some adults, load themselves down with too many activities or too much work, so that they "don't have a minute to think." Youngsters who try to escape continually are often those who lack a sense of their own worth and feel unable to cope with their deepest problems. If a parent can own up to his own escape mechanisms, he will be better able to talk about this with his child, to try to discover what pressures are on him and help him deal with them. Such sharing nourishes parent, child, and home.

Coping with Temptation

As our child gets older, there will be practical problems in connection with drugs for which we will want to prepare ourselves. Will we permit him to go to a party where drugs are likely to be used? If our answer to this is no, how do we plan to prevent this?

By an inquiry before a party to the host or his parents? A mother may want to phone the parent but her child says, "For heaven's sake, you'll make me look like a baby." Or the mother herself just won't feel comfortable asking a woman she doesn't know well, if at all, questions that may indicate she has no faith in this parent's judgment. It is touchy. When parents have worked out a general code of conduct for parties, as discussed in Chapter 3, presumably the situation would not arise.

If drugs appear unexpectedly at a party, if one youngster pulls a reefer out of his pocket, for example, lights up and begins to pass it around, what do we expect our youngster to do? He may feel under considerable pressure to join in. How can he resist, or leave without embarrassment? Discussing such possibilities, working out possible ways to deal with them, is a way of arming a child in advance.

What do we expect our child to do if he knows that a child in his school is using or passing drugs on the school grounds? Sometimes a child will say, "I'll tell you what's happening if you promise not to tell other parents or the school." How should a parent handle that? This kind of request for secrecy comes up about other things, too. Some parents handle it this way. They say, "If I feel it is absolutely necessary for me to take action, I'll discuss my reasons with you and we'll see what we can agree on. Certainly, I would not do anything without telling you first. I hope you trust my judgment enough to tell me what's on your mind, but that decision is up to you." This opens the door to confidences in a way that respects everybody's rights. There is a good possibility that we and our child together can work out a way to take any action that is really needed.

It is a good idea to know—and to make certain our child knows—his school's policy with regard to children who are suspected of or caught using or passing drugs on school grounds.

Children may ask a young teacher whom they like about drugs. What do the teachers in our child's school answer when asked if they have tried or use various drugs? One child reported that his teacher replied, "No comment." It is clear what this connotes to a child. Teachers, like parents, need help in handling children's questions about drugs, especially questions that put them on the spot. What kind of training is our child's school giving teachers to help them deal with this? Does the school system have an effective drug-education program beginning no later than fourth grade?

Sometimes parents delude themselves that they can protect their child by removing drugs from his environment at home, at school, etc., so that he is never exposed to temptation. But this is not possible. School cannot be a jail, and we cannot follow a child around everywhere he goes. Our only protection, and his, will be sound information about drugs and the quality of our relationship with him.

How to Detect Drug Use

Parents frequently ask, "How could I tell if my child were using drugs?" Needless to say, this depends upon the drug and the extent to which it is being used. Can one tell if a child has experimented with marijuana at a party? Probably about as easily as one could tell if the child had experimented with sex at that party; that is to say, not at all, if the child does not want us to know. If a child wants his parents to know about his drug use, he will either tell them or find a way to let them discover it easily for themselves. But we sometimes hear that a child has been deeply involved with drugs for as long as two years without his parents' being aware of it. How can this be?

First of all, many of the symptoms of drug use—carelessness about appearance, moodiness and irritability, frequent phone calls and comings and goings, locked doors, desire for privacy, loss of interest in school, inability to concentrate—can be caused by other problems or just by adolescence.

Second, parents, for a variety of reasons, sometimes need to hide from themselves the possibility that their child is in serious trouble, so they ignore clues that are obvious. Then, too, as a child gets deeper into the drug scene, he becomes very good at covering his tracks.

Herman V. Land, author of *What You Can Do About Drugs and Your Child*, suggests that parents need to be suspicious if there is even a possibility of drug use and search among a child's belongings for evidence. But Drs. Marvin J. Gersh and Iris F. Litt, specialists in adolescent medicine and authors of *The Handbook of Adolescence: A Medical Guide for Parents and Teenagers*, feel this is a disastrous approach, serving only to "drive a wedge between parents and teenagers. Only the symptom will be uncovered, not the cause for it." "We have found," they report, "that the best way to discover if someone is using drugs is to ask him."

Of course, a child who has become dependent upon drugs may not respond with honesty if he feels this will lead his parents to take action he cannot tolerate.

Discovery of drug use is only the first step in helping a child with a drug problem, and the way one goes about it can crucially affect everything that happens after that. If we spy on our child, listen to his conversations, go through his possessions, we break down the trust between us and correspondingly lessen our ability to influence his future behavior.

When there are signs that a child is not functioning well over a period of time in one or more areas, parents should be open about their concern. If they and their child are fortunate enough to communicate well with each other, parents have a good chance of learning what the child feels troubled by. Being in close touch with a child is in itself a good sign. Land reports that "in virtually every case of addiction, there is a breakdown in communication." In families where communication has broken down, new efforts need to be made to restore it (see Chapter 8) and professional help sought if the situation is more than parents can handle alone. If we know our child has become involved with drugs, a safe step would be to consult the family doctor.

If a child is alienated from his parents and their life-style, it will be harder to reach him about drugs and other issues. But if we care about him, we keep trying. He may sometimes reject our advice, as all children occasionally do, yet continue to want and carefully weigh our opinion. We do him a service by answering his questions honestly, telling him how we feel, and listening to him.

11

Planning for When the Children Leave Home

IT MAY SEEM somewhat premature to think about this now. Perhaps our oldest child has only just turned eleven and we have younger children besides. The day when they will all march off, leaving the nest empty, seems far away, its problems hardly pressing. Has the time really come to consider what our lives will be like when they leave us?

Fifty years ago, the average life expectancy of a baby girl was fifty-five years. A mother did not worry about creating a new life for herself after her children were launched because there would presumably be little time left for that. She was considered old at forty. Today, the life expectancy of a baby girl is seventy-four years. It is literally true that child-rearing is only a lovely phase in our lives, and not necessarily the longest one. We may live thirty years or more after our children have essentially left home. That period is too important for us simply to come upon it unawares, unprepared, in a state of emotional crisis. Crisis, because no matter how well we know intellectually that the children will eventually leave home, we are not usually able in imagination to feel what it will be like. For a woman whose main role has been that of "Johnny's mother," it is an identity crisis: Who else am I now when that is not enough?

Right now, the lives of many of us have children at the center. Our children make us feel needed and worthwhile. Our emotions are very much engaged in their concerns. If launching them threatens to create a vacuum nothing else can begin to fill, we will, despite our best intentions, move very slowly to prepare our young birds to fly. The side of us that is afraid of letting them go will hamper the side that nurtures selflessly. We may, although we won't want to, cling. And this will color our children's last years at home and make those years less satisfying than they could be. So, for reasons both selfish and selfless, these next years ought to be a time of getting ready for a new way of life, for us as well as for them, with our preparations muted, not occupying center stage, but conscious, intellectual, emotional, pressing. How?

The Hours of the Day

As our children become more independent, what will fill our hours? New and different possibilities are opening up for women to study and work after they are married and have had children. We need only think in terms of the opportunities of the future instead of the limitations of the past. True, all challenge holds

some fear. Writes Anne Morrow Lindbergh in *Gift from the Sea:*

Who is not afraid of pure space, that breathtaking empty space of an open door?

We all need a focus to our lives besides the children, a serious interest, whether or not we need to earn some of the family income. If earning money is necessary to help with our children's college education or for other reasons, it is even more important to plan so that our efforts will not have to be forever channeled in routine, low-level jobs. But no one should settle for just killing time or keeping busy. Reading all those books we never had the leisure for is not enough. Having endless freedom to be self-indulgent palls when it is endless. A scattered dipping into courses can be a beginning, but it is not a fulfilling occupation.

What are the choices? Someone who already has a serious interest is a step ahead. Others need to think more about it. Is there a field that always held an attraction for us, a skill or talent not yet developed for lack of opportunity or because it used to seem as if women could not do such things? Perhaps a new notion has recently begun to percolate in the back of our head. We can contemplate this and begin to form a design for structuring our life as we have more free time. Then, even if we do not wish to make any major commitments of time or energy now, we can keep a thread going through these next years—the volunteer work we do, the courses we take, some of our reading can be geared toward our purpose. We can maintain membership in a professional society, subscribe to the professional journals in our field, read the new literature, attend conferences, keep abreast of new developments.

If we are thinking about starting our own business, we can begin to learn—from independent reading or courses or friends in business or a part-time job in a similar enterprise—about financing, packaging, pricing, keeping records, insurance, taxes, marketing, distribution, advertising, and so on.

We could begin to learn a new language if that would be helpful in our field. In New York City and many cities in the Southwest with large Spanish-speaking populations, for example, being able to speak this language is an asset in many positions.

In large cities, particularly, courses are available in everything from photography and interior design to such crafts as silversmithing and instrument construction.

Educational Opportunities

If we discover that we need to fill gaps in our education, colleges or universities in forty states and the District of Columbia have continuing education programs with class schedules and accelerated degree programs geared to the needs of the adult woman. Those who want to combine study with homemaking will find that possibilities are proliferating, often with help from federal funds. Tuition varies widely, ranging from very modest to relatively high.

The idea that one has to attend classes on a regular basis or go to school for four consecutive years is being challenged in a number of ways. The State University of New York at Brockport, for example, offers a

Bachelor of Liberal Studies degree for completing a program that includes correspondence courses, private reading, and television classes, plus some classroom attendance at Brockport or elsewhere. The only residence requirement is that one attend an annual three-week seminar in Brockport.

Women who cannot enroll in school on regular schedules will benefit from a huge program for part-time students being launched by the University of California. Its emphasis will be on individual study with books and tapes, supplemented by generous counseling in widely scattered "learning centers." There will undoubtedly be more plans involving independent study in the years to come, although not everyone is likely to be enough of a "superego freak" to be able to work consistently and well on his own.

The University of Missouri at Columbia conducts educational programs for adult women on a statewide basis, utilizing facilities of 116 extension centers and branch campuses. They offer seminars, noncredit short courses, credit courses, independent study programs, and interest and aptitude testing.

Granting credit for a mature woman's life experiences is part of the program advanced by Illinois State University, which offers mature students such services as individual counseling, vocational testing, and assistance in locating remedial courses. Older students are permitted to enroll on a part-time unclassified basis without meeting the usual entrance requirements. And registration priority is given to mothers and working women who need to schedule their classes at convenient times. Their Continuing Education Association is an undergraduate organization for returning students.

Increasingly we hear the word "paraprofessional," meaning a person trained to work alongside the professional doing skilled tasks for which the professional does not have time. Because social problems such as the needs of the young and the aged, the poor and the sick and the troubled are growing faster than the resources available to meet them, paraprofessional training, often on the job, is being offered at an increasing rate in various parts of the country. The New School for Social Research in New York City offers several intensive one-year programs leading to jobs as social work assistant, school psychologist assistant, mental health worker, community health intern, counselor assistant, or community planning intern. The programs combine weekly two-hour seminars at the school with two-day-a-week unpaid jobs as assistants in the field under professional supervision. No previous training or experience is required, and upon completion of the program the student should have acquired a base of knowledge and experience that will enable him to function as a paid or volunteer worker in his chosen field.

More than 400 programs are listed in the U.S. Department of Labor compilation, "Continuing Education Programs and Services for Women." This prospectus is in itself an astonishing indication of how opportunities for women have grown in the past few years. In 1968 its offerings took 104 pages, whereas the 1971 edition requires 167 pages to list all the possibilities.

Learning as a Volunteer

Serious volunteer involvement is another way to

learn, to gain a skill, test an interest, acquire valuable experience for a paid job. One woman who had organized alumnae clubs for her college in various parts of the country was offered the job of assistant dean of admissions for the college's division of continuing education. She was assigned to recruit and interview adults who were returning to school after a ten- to fifteen-year absence.

Others are rewarded for years of political work at the precinct level by jobs in government, like the mother who now has a high-level administrative post on the mayor's staff in New York City after many years of volunteer political activity. Another woman who had been active in the cultural life of her suburban community became executive director of its new cultural center after a summer in a residence workshop to train administrators of the arts.

In some communities, volunteer jobs are particularly varied. They offer a chance to be in contact with different kinds of people and utilize a wide range of skills. In San Francisco, the Volunteer Bureau has asked for swimming aides to help with classes for retarded children, a bridge teacher for psychiatric outpatients, and an artist to draw brochures, letter signs, and design posters for a social service agency. They also need volunteers to teach patients at a convalescent hospital to grow flowers and vegetables, to teach unwed mothers to cook, teen-agers to knit, children at a day-care center to make handicrafts, and Chinese to speak English. They want a hostess for the blood bank, an assistant at the children's art museum, someone with business knowledge to counsel minority businesses, someone to teach a class in Spanish for a hospital staff, someone to make speeches to various groups explaining the work of a philanthropic agency. And the list goes on. It should give us an idea of a service we could perform or a need in our community that we might fill.

Evaluating Skills

But perhaps we are ready to go back to work full-time or part-time and need to evaluate what we might do and what we have to offer a prospective employer. Most women who have not worked outside their homes for several years, if at all, underestimate their potential, according to professionals at Catalyst, a national non-profit organization that is trying to help married women broaden their horizons and utilize their abilities more fully. Rearing children and taking care of a home, they remind us, requires more knowledge, ability, skills, common sense, and judgment than most occupations.

A vocational kit developed by Catalyst suggests that a woman ask herself a long list of questions in order to evaluate her interests and abilities. Is she generally efficient and on time? Do friends, neighbors, fellow members of the P-TA or other organizations for which she has worked feel they can depend upon her?

How well does she get along with others? Is she sensitive to other people's concerns? Is she a good listener? Do people frequently ask for her advice and respect her judgment? Can she work well with people even if she does not like them very much? Is she able to get along with persons whose backgrounds differ from hers? In her life as a housewife and mother she comes into contact with many different types of people

—the clerk at the supermarket, her child's teacher, the repairman, her neighbors, her family. How pleasant and successful are these relationships?

Women tend to believe that the qualities required in the professional and business world are in a different category from those exercised every day by a woman running her home. But diplomacy is diplomacy, whether it involves exercising tact with a teacher or a business associate of our husband's, or a business associate of our own. If we can see a tedious though necessary household or community job through to the end, if we are willing to consider a new way of doing a task we have done dozens of times, we can think of ourself as hard-working and flexible, and be fairly confident that our attributes will not vanish just because someone is paying us to use them. On the other hand, most people are not equally capable in all areas, and the point of this kind of self-evaluation is to help us find out what our strong and weak points are, so that we can arrange our priorities realistically. By thinking in terms of our own life—the people with whom we relate most satis-fyingly, the jobs we do and the kinds of satisfactions we get from various aspects of them—we can get a bet-ter idea of our abilities, our readiness to work, and our value to a prospective employer.

One revealing test is to keep a comprehensive minute-by-minute log of our activities for one week, leaving out nothing. We would include the time we spent in front of the bathroom mirror every day, the minutes we spent looking for a child's socks or helping him with his homework, the period we were on the phone working out plans for the P-TA fair, or just gab-

bing. This way we can judge how much time we really need for ourself, our husband and children, the house, and our other activities. How much of what we do could we give up or delegate to someone else? How much time does that leave us for a paid or volunteer job?

Reasons for Working

What do we want from a job? Is money an immediate and pressing need, or can we enter a field where the compensation is not primarily financial? Could we accept a job with a low starting salary as long as there were good prospects for the future? Or can money be eliminated as a consideration so that we could work as a full- or part-time volunteer? What else is important to us? What do we find stimulating—meeting people, working toward a goal, the exchange of ideas in our field, being of service to others? Says Catalyst:

> Most people have a cluster of experiences, aptitudes and character traits that suit them for more than one occupation. If you worked before, it is natural to think in terms of your past experience, but unless it was substantial and fully satisfying, look closely at what you have done in the intervening years before deciding on your field of work. You may find that you have developed interests and abilities in recent years that have greater significance for the kind of job that is right for you today.

Education, past work experience both paid and unpaid, skills, talents, and general aptitude and ability all need to be weighed and considered.

"We are seeing married women with families returning or starting from scratch to carve out careers in almost every field," writes Jane Schwartz Gould, Director of Placement and Career Planning at Barnard College, in a recent magazine article. Some start out at jobs beneath their ability until they prove themselves, like the woman who began as the secretary to the director of development at a college and one year later became an administrator at the same college.

Many agencies sponsor workshops offering educational and vocational guidance to help women assess their goals and learn of opportunities in work, community service, and education, along with ways and means of achieving them. Back-to-careers programs for mature women are conducted at universities, YWCA's, state employment services, and shopping centers.

Both private and nonprofit personnel organizations are springing up all over the country to help women find part-time jobs and to create more such jobs by doing missionary work among employers. The Distaff Staffers of Washington, D.C., find part-time work for editors, writers, architects, and psychologists among others. New York's Newtime—the new time is a 25-hour workweek, 9:30 to 3:15, five days a week—has found positions for researchers, lawyers, secretaries, fund raisers, and designers and continues to sell business and the professions on the value to them of meeting some women's need for a shorter working day.

Catalyst, in conjunction with the Massachusetts Public Welfare Department, demonstrated the productivity of part-time workers during a two-year pilot project in Boston. Here, fifty college-educated housewives, who had not previously been trained in social work, were hired part-time to take on twenty-five hard-to-fill full-time jobs as caseworkers. Result: They had 89 per cent as many face-to-face contacts with their clients as their full-time counterparts and reduced turnover to one third its usual rate. Although they received some training on the job, their own experience as housewives and mothers contributed toward their understanding of their clients' problems.

The paired job is another way of organizing part-time work that is being tried in pilot projects. On an individual basis, too, some women have been able to convince employers that two people working in tandem can bring more than their share of talent and energy to bear on one full-time position. A partnership arrangement can enrich the classroom when two teachers with complementary skills divide the school day between them. Sometimes paired jobs bring together a senior and junior partner in a position that utilizes their different degrees of skill.

Part-time work is a good solution for many women while the children are still at home, if we can educate more employers to be receptive to the idea. Opportunities are probably best in those fields in which there is a manpower shortage.

Our Marriage

If we are married, we will want at this stage to give thought to nurturing that relationship. As our children need us less and less, will our marriage be able to fill our emotional needs? Marriages are prone to trouble at particular points in time: just after the honeymoon, at the birth of the first child, when the youngest child enters school, and when all of the children leave home. This last is traditionally a time for reassessing the relationship. The marriage changes because its equilibrium is upset. If children have been the main source of mutual interest, the major unifying force, there will be a problem when they leave.

A woman often feels useless and depressed at this time, and there is pressure upon her husband to satisfy her yearning to feel wanted and loved. How will he respond? Because this is a difficult period for her, she may be understandably less capable of thinking clearly about her marriage and working constructively to strengthen it. Married life is a subject too broad and deep for these few pages. Our purpose here is only to stimulate thought about marital satisfactions.

It is helpful if a man and woman are able to take a fresh look at each other and their relationship. Each has surely grown over these several years of marriage. Both partners need to ask themselves: What is different about me, in what ways do I respond differently now from when we were first married? Does my spouse know this about me? How has he (she) changed? Does our relationship acknowledge this growth, or are we still relating to each other as if we were both those youngsters of years past? Can we relate better to each other's new strengths?

This book has explored communication between parents and child. Many of the same principles (see Chapter 8, for example) hold true for communication between man and wife. Can we, do we, talk to each other, have some constructive way of working out differences? The manner in which people communicate is influenced by past successes or failures. Discouragement and lack of hope affect the way we make our needs and wants known, and thereby influence the outcome. Even if only one person in a marriage becomes more sympathetic, more understanding, more supportive of the other, this can generate hope and positive feelings, which have a chance to grow.

Are we ever—often?—alone together? Are we willing to invest time and energy in finding new things to do together, new ways to share time? Frequently, by the time children depart, a man and his wife are, sadly, doing fewer and fewer things jointly. Decisions tend to be made unilaterally: You handle this and I'll take care of that. Yet a marriage benefits from more shared activity, not less.

Sometimes the problem in a marriage is that a man and a woman have allowed their relationship to become stale, devitalized. They have little enthusiasm for each other any more. Women have complained that they can lose ten pounds or completely change their hair style and their husbands will not even notice. They ache, "Look at me, *see* me." Or a man feels his wife treats him like an old shoe, not a *man*.

When married people derive less satisfaction from their relationship than they had hoped for, than they want and need, their disappointment tends to separate them even more. However, it is possible to change the direction of a marriage, sometimes with professional help, sometimes on one's own. Over these next years, while our lives are still full with the comings and goings of our young, we need to pay attention, husband and wife, to each other, to what is going on between us. If the birth of children turns a marriage into a family, when they leave, will it still be a family?

Once we have begun to think ahead about our days and our evenings, whatever we decide to do right away will lead to other things. And the fruit of each will bear many seeds. Just as we determined to give our child's blossoming independence its season, so should we also make time for our own purpose and move along, keeping our new goals in view, when all the while our telephone is still tied up with teen-age gossip.

Bibliography and Suggested Reading

1 Suddenly: Adolescence

Beauvoir, Simone de. *Memoirs of a Dutiful Daughter*. New York: World Publishing Co., 1959.

Blos, Peter. *On Adolescence: A Psychoanaltyic Interpretation*. New York: The Macmillan Company, Free Press Paperback, 1962.

Carroll, Lewis. *Alice's Adventures in Wonderland*. New York: Penguin Books (first published in 1865).

Committee on Adolescence of the Group for the Advancement of Psychiatry. *Normal Adolescence: Its Dynamics and Impact*. New York: Charles Scribner's Sons, 1968.

Erikson, Erik H. *Childhood and Society*. 2d ed. New York: W. W. Norton & Company, Inc., 1963.

———. *Identity: Youth and Crisis*. New York: W. W. Norton & Company, Inc., 1968.

Kiell, Norman. *The Universal Experience of Adolescence*. New York: International Universities Press, Inc., 1964.

Lidz, Theodore. *The Person: His Development Throughout the Life Cycle*. New York: Basic Books, Inc., 1968.

Stone, L. Joseph, and Church, Joseph. *Childhood and Adolescence: A Psychology of the Growing Person*. 2d ed. New York: Random House, 1968.

2 Communicating About Puberty

Arnstein, Helene S. *Your Growing Child and Sex*. In consultation with the Child Study Association of America.

New York: Bobbs-Merrill Co., Inc., 1967.

Breasted, Mary. *Oh! Sex Education.* New York: Praeger Publishers, 1970.

Child Study Association of America. *When Children Ask About Sex.* Revised by Ada Daniels and Mary Hoover. New York, 1969.

Davis, Maxine. *Sex and the Adolescent: A Guide for Young People and Their Parents.* New York: The Dial Press, 1958.

Freud, Martin. *Sigmund Freud: Man and Father.* New York: Vanguard Press, 1958.

Johnson, Eric W. *How to Live Through Junior High School.* New York: J. B. Lippincott Co., 1959.

————. *Love and Sex in Plain Language.* Rev. ed. New York: J. B. Lippincott Co., 1967.

————. *Telling It Straight.* New York: J. B. Lippincott Co., 1970.

LeShan, Eda J. *Sex and Your Teenager: A Guide for Parents.* New York: David McKay Co., Inc., 1969.

Pomeroy, Wardell B., Ph.D. *Boys and Sex: A Long-needed Modern Sexual Guide for Boys.* New York: Delacorte Press, 1968.

————. *Girls and Sex: A Long-needed Modern Sexual Guide for Girls.* New York: Delacorte Press, 1969.

Rabinowitz, Oscar, with Brenton, Myron. "How to Talk to Your Parents About Sex." *Seventeen,* March, 1971.

3 Boy-Girl Relationships

Drury, Michael. *How to Get Along with People.* New York: Doubleday & Co., Inc., 1965.

Duvall, Evelyn Millis, Ph.D. *Today's Teenagers.* New York: Association Press, 1966.

Hechinger, Grace and Fred M. *Teenage Tyranny.* New York: William Morrow & Co., Inc., 1963.

Holt, John. *What Do I Do Monday?* New York: E. P.

Dutton & Co., Inc., 1970.

Paradis, Grace D. and Adrian A. *Your Life: Make It Count.* New York: Funk & Wagnalls, Inc., 1968.

Purtell, Thelma C. *The Intelligent Parents' Guide to Teenagers.* New York: Paul S. Eriksson, Inc., 1961.

Spock, Dr. Benjamin. *A Teenager's Guide to Life and Love.* New York: Simon & Schuster, Inc., 1970.

4 The Struggle Over Limits

Fremon, Suzanne Strait. *Children and Their Parents Toward Maturity.* New York: Harper & Row, 1968.

Redl, Dr. Fritz. *Pre-Adolescents: What Makes Them Tick.* New York: The Child Study Association of America, Inc., 1959.

5 Values

Black, Algernon D. *The First Book of Ethics.* New York: Franklin Watts, Inc.

Bronfenbrenner, Urie. *Two Worlds of Childhood: U.S. and U.S.S.R.* New York: Russell Sage Foundation, 1970.

Hunt, Morton. "The Gentle Art of Understanding Your Parents." *Seventeen*, May 1970.

Keniston, Kenneth. "Youth and Violence: The Contexts of Moral Crisis." In *Moral Education*. Cambridge, Mass.: Harvard University Press, 1970.

Kohlberg, Lawrence. "Education for Justice: A Modern Statement of the Platonic View." In *Moral Education*. Cambridge, Mass.: Harvard University Press, 1970.

Lukas, J. Anthony. *Don't Shoot—We Are Your Children!* New York: Random House, 1971.

Marin, Peter, and Cohen, Allan Y. *Understanding Drug Use: An Adult's Guide to Drugs and the Young.* New York: Harper & Row, 1971.

Reich, Charles A. "The Limits of Duty." *The New Yorker*, June 19, 1971.

Roiphe, Ann Richardson. "The Family Is Out of Fashion." *The New York Times Magazine*, August 15, 1971.

6 Changing Attitudes Toward School

Gesell, Arnold, M.D.; Ilg, Frances L., M.D.; and Ames, Louise B., Ph.D. *Youth: The Years from Ten to Sixteen*. New York: Harper & Row, 1956.

Holt, John. *What Do I Do Monday?* New York: E. P. Dutton & Co., Inc., 1970.

Kagan, Jerome. "A Conception of Early Adolescence." *Daedalus* 100 no. 4, Fall 1971.

Lurie, Ellen. *How to Change the Schools: A Parents' Action Handbook on How to Fight the System*. New York: Random House, 1970.

Martin, Edward C. "Reflections on the Early Adolescent in School." *Daedalus* 100 no. 4, Fall 1971.

Silberman, Charles E. *Crisis in the Classroom: The Remaking of American Education*. New York: Random House, 1970.

7 Everyday Health Guide

Burton, Benjamin T., Ph.D. *Heinz Handbook of Nutrition: A Comprehensive Treatise on Nutrition in Health and Disease*. New York: McGraw-Hill Book Co., 1959.

Englebardt, Stanley L. "If Your Child Has Acne." *Parents' Magazine*, October 1970.

Fisher, Patty, and Bender, Arnold. *The Value of Food*. London: Oxford University Press, 1970.

Gersh, Marvin J., M.D., and Litt, Iris M., M.D. *The Handbook of Adolescence: A Medical Guide for Parents and Teen-agers*. New York: Stein and Day, Inc., 1971.

Katz, Marcella. *Vitamins, Food and Your Health*. Public Affairs Pamphlet no. 465, 1971.

King, Charles Glen, and Lam, Gwen. *Personality "Plus" Through Diet: Foodlore for Teen-agers*. Public Affairs

Pamphlet no. 299, 1960.

Levine, Milton I., M.D., and Seligmann, Jean H. *Your Overweight Child*. New York: World Publishing Co., 1970.

Mason, Gussie, with Wilson, Jean Sprain. *Help Your Child Lose Weight*. New York: Hawthorn Books, Inc., 1969.

McKay, Stella. *Your Child's Health from Birth to Adolescence*. New York: Doubleday and Co., Inc., 1965.

President's Council on Physical Fitness. *Vigor: A Complete Exercise Plan for Boys 12 to 18*. Washington, D.C.: U.S. Government Printing Office.

————. *Vim: A Complete Exercise Plan for Girls 12 to 18*. Washington, D.C.: U.S. Government Printing Office.

Rossman, Isadore, M.D. *Nutrition for Your Family's Health*. New York: The Emily Post Institute, Inc., 1963.

Seely, Janet E.; Zuskin, Eugenija; and Bouhuys, Arend. "Cigarette Smoking: Objective Evidence for Lung Damage in Teenagers." John B. Pierce Foundation and Department of Medicine, Yale University School of Medicine. *Science*, May 14, 1971.

Shultz, Gladys Denny. *The Successful Teen-Age Girl*. New York: J. B. Lippincott Co., 1968.

Van Atta, Winifred. "A Program for Overweight Teenagers." *Parents' Magazine*, November, 1968.

Watt, Bernice K., and Merrill, Annabel L. *Composition of Foods: Raw, processed, prepared*. Washington, D.C.: United States Department of Agriculture. Revised, 1963.

Wilkes, Edward T., M.D. *The Family Guide to Teenage Health*. New York: Ronald Press Co., 1958.

8 Adolescent Misery

Baruch, Dorothy. *How to Live with Your Teen-ager*. New York: McGraw-Hill Book Co., 1953.

Bashkirtseff, Marie. *The Journal of a Young Artist*. New York: E. P. Dutton & Co., 1926.

Benedict, Ruth. *Patterns of Culture*. New York: The New American Library, Inc., 1934.

Bienvenue, Millard J., Sr. "Why They Can't Talk to Us." *The New York Times Magazine*, September 14, 1969.

Frank, Anne. *The Diary of a Young Girl*. New York: Doubleday & Co., Inc., 1952.

Ginott, Dr. Haim G. *Between Parent and Child: New Solutions to Old Problems*. New York: The Macmillan Company, 1969.

———. *Between Parent and Teenager*. New York: The Macmillan Company, 1965.

Mill, John Stuart. *Autobiography*. Library of Liberal Arts, 1957.

Rice, John A. *I Came Out of the Eighteenth Century*. New York: Harper & Bros., 1942.

Senn, Milton J. E., M.D., and Solnit, Albert J., M.D. *Problems in Child Behavior and Development*. Philadelphia: Lea and Febiger, 1968.

9 Money: Earning It and Having It

Frank, Lawrence K. and Mary. *Your Adolescent at Home and in School*. New York: The Viking Press, 1956.

10 Drugs and Other Escape Mechanisms

Child Study Association of America. *You, Your Child and Drugs*. New York: The Child Study Press, 1971.

Coles, Robert, M.D.; Brenner, Joseph H., M.D; and Meagher, Dermet. *Drugs and Youth—Medical, Psychiatric and Legal Facts*. New York: Liveright Publishing Corp., 1970.

Gallagher, Dorothy. "Johnny Cash: 'I'm Growing, I'm Changing, I'm Becoming.' " *Redbook*, August 1971.

Gersh, Marvin J., M.D., and Litt, Iris J., M.D. *The Handbook of Adolescence: A Medical Guide for Parents and Teenagers. New York: Stein and Day, Inc., 1971.

Goode, Erich. The Marijuana Smokers. New York: Basic Books, Inc., 1970.

Greenberg, Harvey R., M.D. What You Must Know About Drugs. New York: Scholastic Book Services, 1970.

Grinspoon, Lester, M.D. Marihuana Reconsidered. Cambridge, Mass.: Harvard University Press, 1971.

Land, Herman V. What You Can Do About Drugs and Your Child. New York: Pocket Books, 1971.

Marin, Peter, and Cohen, Allan Y. Understanding Drug Use: An Adult's Guide to Drugs and the Young. New York: Harper & Row, 1971.

National Clearing House for Drug Abuse Information. A Federal Source Book: Answers to the Most Frequently Asked Questions About Drug Abuse.

National Institute of Mental Health. Alcohol and Alcoholism.

11 Planning for When the Children Leave Home

Benjamin, Lois. So You Want to Be a Working Mother! New York: McGraw-Hill Book Co., 1966.

Catalyst. Westchester Project Vocational Kit: Designed for Family Women Who Wish to Begin or Resume Work. New York: Catalyst, 1971.

Friedan, Betty. The Feminine Mystique. New York: W. W. Norton & Company, Inc., 1963.

Gould, Jane Schwartz. "Our Changing Careers." Barnard Alumnae Magazine, Winter, 1971.

Lindbergh, Anne Morrow. Gift from the Sea. New York: Pantheon Books, 1955.

Peterson, James A. Married Love in the Middle Years. New York: Association Press, 1968.

Schwartz, Felice N.; Shifter, Margaret H.; and Gillotti, Susan. How to Go to Work When Your Husband Is

Against It, Your Children Aren't Old Enough and There's Nothing You Can Do Anyhow. New York: Simon & Schuster, Inc., 1972.

Schwartz, Jane. *Part-Time Employment: Employer Attitudes on Opportunities for the College-Trained Woman, Report of a Pilot Project.* New York: Alumnae Advisory Center, Inc., 1964.

Scobey, Joan, and McGrath, Lee Parr. *Creative Careers for Women: A Handbook of Sources and Ideas for Part-Time Jobs.* New York: Essandess Special Editions, 1968.

Women's Bureau. *Continuing Education Programs and Services for Women.* Rev. ed. Washington, D.C.: U.S. Department of Labor, 1971.

———. *Handbook on Women Workers.* Washington, D.C.: U.S. Department of Labor, 1969.

———. *Jobfinding Techniques for Mature Women.* Washington, D.C.: U.S. Department of Labor, 1970.

———. *Job Training Suggestions for Women and Girls.* Washington, D.C.: U.S. Department of Labor, 1970.

Additional Reading

Albrecht, Margaret. *Parents and Teen-agers: Getting Through to Each Other.* New York: Parents' Magazine Press, 1972.

Gilbert, Sara D. *Three Years to Grow: Guidance for Your Child's First Three Years.* New York: Parents' Magazine Press, 1972.

Hoover, Mary B. *The Responsive Parent: Meeting the Realities of Parenthood Today.* New York: Parents' Magazine Press, 1972.

Mogal, Doris P. *Character in the Making: The Many Ways Parents Can Help the School-age Child.* New York: Parents' Magazine Press, 1972.

Neisser, Edith G. *Primer for Parents of Preschoolers.* New York: Parents' Magazine Press, 1972.

Index

281